Len

It's Not What I'm Eating... It's What's Eating Me!

Written by Len Dippold and
Velma (Daffy) Dippold

Cecilia
Thank you

Lorelei Edgecomb
(Lori Aranon)

The UNBOUND Bookmaker

The Dippolds have been married for more than fifty years, with more than twenty-five of those years in recovery from the family disease of alcoholism. They live in a house more than a hundred years old in upstate New York. Their business website is www.drugfreequizbee.com.

ISBN-13: 978-1461069324/ISBN-10: 1-461-06932-7

Cover illustration by Carol A. Phillips
www.herbwoman1313@aol.com

Edited and typeset by The Unbound Bookmaker
www.unboundbookmaker.com

Dedication

Delos Adams, who served with the North in the Civil War, had two sons and three daughters. One of the sons, John Edward Adams, married Elizabeth Weber, and they had two daughters. The youngest daughter was Dorothy (Dot) Mabel Adams; she was born on September 13th, 1908, the same year that the Wright brothers first flew one mile. Dot's sister, Marian, was just two years older than Dot, and she was a good friend as well as a sister. Dot took the name of her mother for a confirmation name, married Leonard George Dippold, and became Dorothy Mabel Elizabeth Adams Dippold.

Dot's mother, Elizabeth, had suffered rheumatic fever as a child and was never again blessed with good health. When Dot was about nine years old, she took a nap with her mother. When Dot woke up, her mother had died of heart failure. This left John Adams a widower with two little girls to raise. For a man who needed to make a living for his family, this would be a difficult chore at best. John worked as a finish painter for typewriters, which were hand-painted in those days, the days before there were computers and electric typing machines. In a time when education for women was limited, Marian went to normal school and became a teacher while Dorothy was trained in shorthand and typing to become a secretary. Dorothy made many friends and was much loved by her friends and family. She was also, by many opinions, a very beautiful woman both physically and spiritually. Her understanding of human nature made her a natural psychologist, and she could see that alcoholism was destroying members of her family.

John had a brother, Willie, who was a "street alcoholic," and John was prone to excessive drinking himself. Eventually, Uncle Willie died in the streets without friends or family nearby, a bottle at his side. Both Dorothy and her sister were aware that their father drank too much and vowed to never marry alcoholics, but both did.

Dorothy first met her future husband, Len, in grade school. Although they were in the same grade, they were in different rooms and had no real relationship at that time. They met again on a blind date where Len saw her and decided that she was for him. Yes, she was a beauty. Len was a skinny man and his first son had the same ultra-slim build. Len was also an alcoholic in the making. His son took after him there, too.

Dot lived through the era of Prohibition and fondly remembered the days of the Charleston and speakeasies. It is worth noting that Prohibition, which was supposed to cure the problem of alcoholism, resulted in the rise of gangsters. Remember Al Capone? He was often welcome in high society as the supplier of booze, which made parties more fun. The alcohol never did stopped flowing. Horror stories are told of blindness and even death resulting from drinking wood alcohol, "bathtub gin," and the like. But alcohol and alcoholism just couldn't be legislated away. Even an otherwise law-abiding person such as Dot ignored drinking laws.

Dot and Len eloped at the urging of Dot's sister and "Uncle Wes." Marian and Wes wanted to get married, but Marian was afraid to do it because of her father, who she was sure would object strenuously. So little sister, who was seen as daddy's favorite, was sold the famous "bill of goods." After their father calmed down, Marian and Wes were also married.

Dot's first-born son, Len Jr., was born in 1935, and a second child came ten years later. John, the second son, was killed at the age of twelve in a hunting accident. Dot never fully recovered from his death, but in her extraordinary way, she kept everything going as usual.

Shortly after Len Jr. came home from the army, he married Velma, his lifelong mate. With the well-earned nickname "Daffy," she became the daughter Dot had always wanted. Daffy and Dot were very close, so close that they considered each other mother and daughter. In a period of four years, Len and Daffy had three children, who came to love their grandma. But like so many kids, it was easier to say Baba than Grandma, so Dot became Baba not only to her grandkids but also to the neighbors, friends, church members, and most everyone who knew her well. She went to see her grandkids after work every day and was known to all the children in the area as Baba. One day the neighbor kids were discussing who had the most and best things, like "you have a swing set, your family has a new car, you have eight Barbies," etc. The matter was put to rest when one of the kids said, "Yeah, but you've got a Baba!" End of discussion.

She lived to see man land on the moon, her grandkids have children of their own, and her son get into recovery from alcoholism. Her husband died at sixty, but Baba lived to the age of eighty-two, probably because she had a healthy lifestyle and because she was so busy taking care of her family. Her mind never slipped. She did, however, suffer from ulcers for many years and used many bottles of Maalox. One day when she was contemplating her life with an alcoholic father, husband, and son, she responded to a comment about the food she was eating and her ulcer with the statement: "It's not what I'm eating . . . it's what's eating me!"

As a daughter, wife, and mother to a family struggling with multiple generations addicted to alcohol, Baba showed remarkable courage, stamina, and patience. Her patience has been rewarded by seeing the addiction cycle in her family break. We hope her example gives the same courage, stamina, and patience to those family members who are "holding it all together" in families that also struggle with addiction.

And so, with a tear in the eye and love in the heart, we dedicate this book as a memorial to the finest amateur psychologist and the most exemplary human being we have ever known, our Baba.

iii

Contents

Part III: How We Made It

Foreword:
Are You Ready?

The world's greatest two-letter word sentence:
"If it is to be, it is up to me."

∿

Love roller coasters? Hate roller coasters? Why?

There are different types of roller coasters. They go up and up and up and suddenly tip and go back down at breakneck speeds. Or down and whip around. Some go upside down, even whirl up and around in a loop. Roller coasters are thrilling, scary, and keep the rider on edge.

Some of us love roller coasters and some of us hate them. The excitement they generate can be addicting. The ups and downs and twists and turns and constant state of imbalance can make a smooth ride seem dull and humdrum.

It might seem logical that folks who get out of stressful, even nightmarish, situations would treasure the peace of a placid life. For some this is so, but others miss the chaos and tension they are accustomed to. The excitement of living in an alcoholic—or otherwise addicted—family has been described as riding a roller coaster in and out of hell. It is sometimes reminiscent of a war zone.

A few years ago, someone noted that Posttraumatic stress disorder (PTSD) was most observed in Vietnam veterans and adult children of alcoholics. PTSD in Vietnam vets made sense. But in children of alcoholics?

According to the PTSD Information Center:

After a trauma or life-threatening event it is common to have upsetting memories of what happened, to have trouble sleeping, to feel jumpy, or to lose interest in things you used to enjoy. For some people these reactions do not go away on their own, or may even get worse over time. These people may have Posttraumatic Stress Disorder.

Posttraumatic Stress Disorder (PTSD) is an anxiety disorder that can occur after you have been through a traumatic event. A traumatic event is something horrible and scary that you see or that happens to you. During this type of event, you think that your life or others' lives are in danger. You may feel afraid or feel that you have no control over what is happening.[1]

One wouldn't think that life in an alcoholic family would be as stressful as going to war. But in many ways the stress is the same, never knowing when a roadside bomb may go off.

Children have very little power in family situations. Families where addiction is present often suffer neglect and/or abuse. A child in an addicted family may feel powerless and afraid—afraid for himself or herself and for the other parent or siblings, and even for the addicted parent. Feelings of powerlessness and fear over a long period of time are bound to have some effect on the children involved. This fits in with the description of Posttraumatic Stress Disorder.

Even though the child, now an adult, may be long out of the situation, flashbacks can occur. So can an undefined, uneasy feeling, especially when it is triggered by an event similar to or bringing back memories of trauma suffered as a child. Because it is familiar to them, children of alcoholics often marry alcoholics or other children of alcoholics and the cycle continues.

There are ways of navigating the minefields of the alcoholism, some better than others. One way involves controlling your thoughts: Francis Bacon said, "For also knowledge itself is power."[2] These days we simply say, "knowledge is power." And Einstein is often quoted as saying, "Imagination is everything. It is a preview of coming attractions." We often have overactive imaginations, mostly expecting the worst of what's coming. We practice the power of negative thinking. We have the power to change our thinking and imagining, although it's not easy. There is help. Thousands, maybe

---

[1]United States Department of Veterans Affairs, "National Center for Posttraumatic Stress Disorder," http://ptsd.va.gov.

[2]Francis Bacon, *Meditationes Sacrae* (1597).

millions of us, have found freedom and joy in spite of outside conditions. So don't give up.

Remember, the journey of a thousand miles begins with a single step. Did Einstein say that, too? No, but he might have if somebody hadn't beat him to it.

We have placed quotations from wise people at the beginning of each chapter so that we can humbly learn from others as we seek to make our lives and the lives of our families better. Also, at the end of each chapter we have placed some jokes in the hope that even though this is a very serious subject, you can learn to laugh and your burden will be lighter.

So what's stopping you from taking that first step off the roller coaster and out of the war zone?

I haven't had any experience with UFOs, but paranormal life seems to be all around me...I grew up on the lower east side of New York.
Attributed to David Duchovny
(Could this also be said of growing up in the addicted family?)

Part I: For the Co-Dependents

If It's His Problem, Why Do *I* Have the Ulcer?

Wine is a mocker, strong drink a raging:
and whosoever is deceived thereby is not wise.
Proverbs 20:1

Be not hasty in the spirit to be angry:
for anger resteth in the bosom of fools.
Ecclesiastes 7:9

~

If it's his problem, why do *I* have the ulcer?

Good question. How could someone else's problem cause me to be sick? It's a fact that co-dependents (those who live with alcoholics or other addicts) have a high incidence of stress-related disorders.

You ask, "If it's my problem, is there anything I can do about it—other than drowning my husband in the bathtub?" The answer is YES! Read on.

The drinking or other addictive behavior of a spouse—or parent or child—can be devastating to anyone's mental health. Since our mental state has a great effect on our physical well being, it's no surprise that someone engulfed in the stress of living with an alcoholic could develop an ulcer.

So then, you ask, if I'm the crazy sick one, is my alcoholic husband OK? No one would say that the alcoholic is OK. Far from it. But consider this: Father Joseph C. Martin,[3] a Catholic priest and a recovering alcoholic, educated people struggling with alcoholism. He said, "If you want to know if a man is an alcoholic, LOOK AT HIS WIFE!"[4]

---

[3] Father Joseph C. Martin (1924–2009), ordained 1948, Diocese of Baltimore.
[4] As qtd. in *Chalk Talk*, a book and movie presentation that imparted useful information on alcoholism/addiction in an interesting way, often with humor.

You might be surprised to know that sometimes the behavior of the wife or husband is more bizarre than that of the alcoholic.

This happened long ago:

It was a cold winter night. I had been in the house with the kids for days and really needed a change of scene. My husband went out drinking but promised to be back by ten o'clock so we could go out for a while, as we had someone to watch the kids.

Ten o'clock came and went, as did eleven, twelve, one, and two. I was getting more nervous, worried and stressed with each passing hour. What had happened? He had promised to be home. Was he smashed and lying in a ditch somewhere? He was smashed all right, as I found out when he staggered in somewhere between three and four.

When I saw that he was alive and uninjured and totally bombed out of his mind, I reacted. I whined, accused, ranted, raved, and when I got no reaction, became furious and began punching and smacking him until he responded in a drunken stupor, but he was sufficiently lucid that I understood him perfectly. He said if I continued what I was doing, he would hit back. Although I was consumed with rage, some rational part of me acknowledged that I was no match for him, even in that state. So I stopped and he promptly passed out on the bed, to sleep 'til very late in the morning. In contrast, I tossed and turned and slept fitfully. Awake early, I looked in the mirror and could hardly believe what I saw. A healing cold sore that was the size of a small zit the night before was the size of a dime and festering.

The incident—actually, my reaction to the incident—had triggered strong, even toxic emotions. My anger had poisoned me! Although I was aware of what my anger had done, I was clueless as to what I could do about it.

This happened many years ago. I could tell you numerous horror stories of the alcoholic family and you might relate to some of them. After a very long time, I began to realize that even if I got rid of this alcoholic, I would probably end up with another one—or some other wackadoo—and if I wanted to attract another type of person, I would need to become another type of person myself.

Daffy, Al-Anon member

In writing this book, it is our hope to give you useful information gained from our experience in addiction and recovery that may enable you to see more clearly what is going on, what you are up against, and how you might make changes in yourself that will make your life better, regardless of what anyone else is doing.

◁ ☺ ▷

IF YOU CAN...

If you can start the day without caffeine,
If you can get going without pep pills,
If you can be cheerful, ignoring aches and pains,
If you can resist complaining and boring people with your troubles,
If you can eat the same food every day and be grateful for it,
If you can understand when your loved ones are too busy to give you any time,
If you can take criticism and blame without resentment,
If you can ignore a friend's limited education and never correct him,
If you can resist treating a rich friend better than a poor friend,
If you can conquer tension without medication,
If you can relax without liquor,
If you can sleep without the aid of drugs,
Then you are probably the family dog.

Growing Up in an Alcoholic Family

For thy love is better than wine.
Song of Solomon 1:2
(some folks should stick to love)

I don't think of all the misery, but about the
beauty that still remains.
Anne Frank[5]

Say you are well or all is well with you
And God shall hear your words and make them come true.
Ella Wheeler Wilcox[6]

❧

It's been said that the spouse of an alcoholic feels helpless, but the child of an alcoholic IS helpless.

Many of us can relate to the chaos of a dysfunctional family. All families are probably dysfunctional to some degree. Not all dysfunctional families are alcoholic, but all alcoholic families ARE dysfunctional. You may relate to this story.

By the time I was a teenager, I felt lost, misunderstood, disillusioned, and alone.

I did not imagine anyone else was going through what I was. I now know my friends' families were abnormal in other ways, but no one seemed to be experiencing the chaos that existed in my family. For a while, my high school had a drug counselor. It was helpful to talk to her, but there

---

[5] Anne Frank, *The Diary of a Young Girl: The Definitive Edition*, ed. Otto Frank and Mirjam Pressler (Doubleday, 1995), 211.
[6] Ella Wheeler Wilcox (1850–1919), American writer and poet.

were few times when we could speak privately. My church youth leaders were aware of the alcoholism in my family and were very sympathetic, but they were clueless as to how to help.

Since age three, I had wanted to become a nurse. I investigated nursing schools and was ready to sign up with the Air Force, which would pay for my RN degree. Even in high school, I was looking for an escape route. In my senior year, I met someone who seemed like an ideal mate. Because of the dysfunction in my family, I hadn't a clue as to what an ideal mate might be. This young man, like me, was trying to escape a family situation—in his case, abuse.

I decided to get married, thinking I could still get my education. This did not happen because my husband deemed it unimportant and refused to help in any way. Five years and four children later, I was a single parent with no marketable skills and was unequipped to deal with life in general. Although I enrolled in a nearby college, I did poorly due to dyslexia and an inability to juggle my responsibilities. It's amazing that I passed anything.

I moved to another state, stayed at home, trying to parent four children, including a mentally challenged son who sometimes had violent episodes. When all the children were in school, I enrolled in a technical school and received my LPN license. Working in nursing homes exposed me to some issues that turned me off to the nursing profession.

I then spent almost five years working at a theme park. While there, I tried to also be a full-time student, struggling with my learning disability, racking up a few F's and incompletes and some passing grades. More than twenty years after high school graduation, I finally was able to "walk down the aisle" and receive my degree, not with honors, just barely making it, but I MADE IT!

A few years into my marriage and with two children, my family had an intervention for my dad. No one really thought it would work, but thankfully it did. He went into a local rehab for forty-two days. While there, he had a spiritual experience that took away all his desire to drink. Since then, he has tried to help other alcoholics and their families. My mom, after feeling that her husband's drinking was not HER problem, got to Al-Anon. Our family is still not the Waltons or the Brady Bunch, but we are experiencing the sanity and serenity that we were missing while I was growing up.

Through programs like Al-Anon, I have learned that my life does not need to be chaotic. I have grown spiritually and now have a better understanding of God and the peace one can have, even when it seems one's world is falling apart.

Had the academic and spiritual leaders of my youth steered me to programs like Alateen, I might have gained an understanding that I was not responsible for my dad's drinking or my chaotic family, but only for my own choices. Perhaps most importantly, I would've met others in my situation and learned I was not alone. Had I gotten help earlier, I believe I would've avoided many of the negative situations of my life, or at least have been better equipped to handle them.

Lori, Al-Anon member

◁ ☺ ▷
OLD FARMER'S ADVICE

Your fences need to be horse-high, pig-tight, and bull-strong.

Life is simpler when you plow around the stump.

A bumblebee is considerably faster than a John Deere tractor.

Words that soak into your ears are whispered...not yelled.

Meanness don't just happen overnight.

Forgive your enemies; it messes up their heads.

Do not corner something that you know is meaner than you.

It don't take a very big person to carry a grudge.

You cannot unsay a cruel word.

Every path has a few puddles.

When you wallow with pigs, expect to get dirty.

12

Points to Ponder

It's not the things people don't know that hurts them,
it's the things they know that ain't so.
Will Rogers[7]

~

There is a sickness people often get if they live in hot and swampy places. It seems to be worse when people leave their windows open at night. It must be caused by the bad air. That's why it's called "mal-aria."

The best remedy for illness is to get rid of excess blood by "bleeding" the patient.

Autism is caused by mothers who are cold and unfeeling toward their children. They were known as "refrigerator mothers."

Don't laugh. All these were accepted as fact by the "experts" and the public. There was some truth to them. Leaving windows open at night did seem to have a relationship to malaria, but it wasn't the air. It was the mosquitoes that came in with the air.

Getting rid of some blood did help some patients. High blood pressure can be brought down this way. But overall it may have done more harm than good and it fell out of favor.

While the cause of autism is not fully known, what is known is that it is NOT a result of the mother's attitude. What a sad thing that autistic children were institutionalized and their mothers lived with a load of guilt for it, thinking that they were responsible.

Have you ever had surgery, even minor surgery, and been given a form to sign that you understand the things that can go wrong with your procedure? Your toes may curl up, your eyeballs may fall

---

[7] Will Rogers (1879–1935), American cowboy, comedian, humorist.

out, your saliva may turn green, your armpits may sprout acres of long curly hair. Then, as if this explains everything, comes the bottom line: surgery is not an exact science. Well, neither is addiction!

Keep an open mind. Albert Einstein was the greatest scientist of our time, maybe of all time. His colleagues were also great scientists, yet they didn't always agree. They found that sometimes the design of the experiment influences the result, e.g., the nature of light—is it waves or particles? If the best scientists are unable to agree, what would you expect for the rest of us?

The next few chapters will present the idea that alcoholism is a disease, not merely bad behavior. There have been an amazing number of studies on this and some wild disagreement. Were one to read all these studies, it would cause eyestrain, and if sitting on a hard chair, hemorrhoids. And perhaps not much enlightenment.

We suggest you approach this with an open mind and see if you feel that the ideas make sense to you.

◁☺▷

RETIRED MILITARY

Tom was in his early fifties and had just started a second career. However, he just couldn't seem to get to work on time, no matter how hard he tried. Every day he was five, ten, fifteen minutes late. But, he was a good worker and real sharp, so the boss was in a quandary about how to deal with it. Finally, one day he called Tom into his office for a talk.

"Tom, I have to tell you. I like your work ethic. You do a bang-up job, but your being late so often is quite bothersome."

"Yes, I know, boss, and I am working on it."

"Well, good—you are a team player. That's what I like to hear. I know you're retired from the Air Force. What did they say if you came in late there?"

"They said, 'Good morning, General.'"

What Is Alcoholism?

O God, that men should put an enemy in their mouths
to steal away their brains! That we should with joy, pleasance,
revel and applause, transform ourselves into beasts!
Shakespeare, Othello

～

There is more than a little controversy surrounding this idea. How could excessive drinking be anything other than a stupid choice some people make? Most of us are intelligent enough to know a bad choice when we see one and then avoid it. Here's what one recovering alcoholic has to say:

> I visited an old friend who had recently retired from his job. We agreed that he had a great life of golfing and fishing in summer and skiing in winter. Hal and I agree on most things, being similar in background and interests.

> However, on this visit, we came upon an area of disagreement that reflects the feelings of many people who have had the fortune, or misfortune, of working with alcoholics and drug addicts. Hal was head of the parole department in our county before he retired. Many of the clients who passed through his offices were alcoholics and drug users. I am an alcoholic who has been sober for over 25 years. I am convinced that alcoholism is a disease. Hal thinks it is a behavioral and a moral problem.

> Right from the start, I wish to acknowledge that most of the early symptoms of alcoholism manifest themselves as behavior problems. And since alcoholism is a progressive disease, the behavior doesn't get any better, but instead gets worse as

time passes. But that's enough of my thoughts for the time being. This is the story as Hal sees it.

Several surveys have asked inmates if they had been drinking or drugging at the time of their crime. Over half the prison inmates said, "YES, do you think I would've done that if I'd been sober?!"

Now it has come to pass that many lawyers are trying to use the "they made me do it" argument with regard to alcohol and other drugs, as if the drug were responsible for the crime. (Did you ever see a bottle of vodka hold up a bank?) This is the scenario that Hal was seeing in his work.

Inmates were showing up, blaming the use of some substance for their behavior, using this excuse and the promise of continuing treatment as a basis for being released on parole. As soon as the prisoners were released—or shortly after—they reverted to their old behavior, including the use of drugs of one sort or another. So being head of the parole department, Hal was constantly reminded that these parolees were using the "my behavior will be better without ____ drug, so let me out and I will show you" approach.

Then it fell upon Hal and his department to face the continued bad behavior of these people and they (the parole officers) soon decided it would have been better if the former inmates had remained locked up instead of being released to the public domain. Or to put it another way, they used the "disease" excuse to get out but then did nothing to treat the "disease," so it really was just a convenient excuse to get out. Their bad behavior didn't change. The inmates had found that lying to the parole board usually worked, so they did it without any intention of getting help. (Let's face it—these were not the straightest arrows in the quiver to start with, so why should we expect them to hit OUR target?) Is it any wonder that people in law enforcement have their doubts? What do they see? What basis do they have for making a judgment?

As a quick reminder, denial is the first symptom of alcoholism, and it's also the one that must be dealt with first. I see no indication that denial has been handled with the convicts, so I see no reason why they should be expected to get treatment in a serious way if denial has not been broken and a bottom hit. For many people, time in jail would be rock bottom, but this is just not true of everybody.

Here's how it looks to a recovering alcoholic involved in working with teenagers:

> When I was early in my recovery, I spent a lot of time working on issues with high school-aged kids. (I had started my own drinking career at the age of fourteen as a high school freshman.) We were aware of a small group of local high school students who were recovering from addiction. These kids felt the need to have a place to meet for support during the day. They liked to get together for mutual support at lunchtime, but the cafeteria, with classmates at the next table giving detailed accounts of drugs and parties, was not the place for some already fragile teens to discuss their problems.
>
> A few of us had been made aware of the situation and went to the local school official who had the job of dealing with addiction problems in the schools. (Parents and advocates for the students had appointed him, and he took his position seriously and with compassion.) He arranged a meeting with the principal of the school in question, and the principal grudgingly gave the kids a meeting room. He did, however, grumble about it, and we knew it would never have happened if we had not had the support of "downtown" with us. This attitude of not wanting to jump right in to help his students bothered us, so we thought it wise to find out why, since we would probably have to deal with him in the future. We found out that his wife had run off with a recovering alcoholic, and he just thought it (recovery from a disease) was a big phony act to have an excuse to steal another man's wife. Wow! What a weird leap that was. But this kind of thinking is sometimes real and must be dealt with.

AMA AND THE EMERGENCY ROOM DOCTORS

In the 1950s the American Medical Association declared that alcoholism was a disease—sometimes called Jellinek's Disease after Dr. Elvin Morton Jellinek,[8] who gave alcoholism an accurate but very long medical definition. However, some MDs, and in particular those that work in emergency rooms, see the broken bodies that are a result of drunkenness and think that if only people didn't drink, this would never happen. Clearly, many MDs still think of alcoholism

---

[8] Elvin Morton Jellinek (1890–1963), biostatistician, physiologist, alcoholism researcher.

as a behavioral problem rather than a disease. Under these conditions, it is hard to think it was a disease that caused the drinking. Of course it sometimes is just too much partying or a binge and has nothing to do with alcoholism. But if the same individual keeps showing up with stab wounds from a bar fight, injuries in a DWI accident, or injuries from falling from a ladder at 9:00 a.m. (and is reeking of booze), even the ER docs might suspect something more than some bad choices.

HOW ABOUT ONE MORE IDEA?

People learn how to handle children based on the way they were raised. If dad beats them a lot, that is the way it is done. They don't know any other way. When they grow up and have kids of their own, how are they going to treat them? Probably the same way they were treated. After all, "If I made it, and I am OK, then what is wrong with bringing up my kids this way? And besides, what other way do I know?"

By the same token, if mom or dad drank a lot to have fun, relax, and deal with their trouble, how do you think I will deal with mine? "I learned from my own folks, and I love them so this must be the way things are done."

This, in a nutshell, is what the behaviorists say about alcoholism, since it tends to run in families. Diabetes also tends to run in families. Is this behavior related too? Could be, if we think that we usually eat the same foods, put on the same pounds, etc., that our parents did. But we can show abnormal body chemistry for diabetes. So we know it is a disease with a genetic link to our parents, but nevertheless, it is a disease. Let's leave it there for now.

Dogs feel very strongly that they should always go with you in the car, in case the need should arise for them to bark violently at nothing right in your ear.
Dave Barr

I loathe people who keep dogs. They are cowards who haven't got the guts to bite people themselves.
Author Unknown

To sit with a dog on a hillside on a glorious afternoon is to be back in Eden, where doing nothing was not boring—it was peace.
Milan Kunder

Dogs have given us their absolute all. We are the center of their universe. We are the focus of their love and faith and trust. They serve us in return for scraps. It is without a doubt the best deal man has ever made.
Roger Caras

I wonder if other dogs think poodles are members
of a weird religious cult.
Rita Rudner

If you can look at a dog and not feel vicarious excitement
and affection, you must be a cat.
Author Unknown

The Tale of the Rat

It is cheering to see that the rats are still around—
the ship is not sinking.
Eric Hoffer[9]

Everywhere in the world is this marvelous balance
of beauty and disgust, magnificence and rats.
Ralph Waldo Emerson[10]

～

Most of us are not rat lovers, but we have learned to respect the information that can be obtained from rat research. So what tale do the rats tell us?

A few years ago, a young cancer researcher, Virginia E. Davis, was doing research on brain cancer down in Houston, Texas, where road rage sometimes results in gunfire. Now, it is not easy to obtain fresh brain tissue for experimentation, even with Texas road rage. But the main source of fresh brain tissue does come from recently deceased individuals. Now it seems that, although people are dying frequently, not too many are donating their brains to science. Therefore, the main supply had to come from the street people, the winos who had passed away and had become unclaimed corpses in the morgue. During the examination of these tissue samples, Virginia found a substance known as tetrahydroisoquinoline, or THIQ.

Now this substance was not new to medical science, and it was known to be a highly addicting substance found in the brains of heroin addicts. It had been discarded by the medical field for human use as a painkiller because of its highly addictive properties. This was an interesting discovery, though, and Virginia made a comment to her peers about the large number of heroin addicts

[9] Eric Hoffer (1920–1983), U.S. writer.
[10] Ralph Waldo Emerson (1803–1882), U.S. poet, lecturer, essayist.

among the street people. They said that this was "not likely," as the street folks could hardly afford their cheap wine, let alone far more expensive heroin.

And so began a new line of research. Experimentation and research led to some interesting results. To simplify something very complex, let's just say that when a person drinks alcohol, some of it goes quickly to the blood stream. It is this action that makes one intoxicated, and it is the basis for blood alcohol tests used to determine driver sobriety.

Some of the alcohol is digested in a routine way. The alcohol is broken down into acetic acid, which then breaks down into carbon dioxide and water. This happens in both alcoholics and in normal social drinkers. On the way to becoming CO_2 and H_2O, there is an intermediate step, which is the formation of acetaldehyde. Now this is nasty stuff, as it is a first cousin to formaldehyde—historically known as embalming fluid. It can kill as well as preserve tissue. But this not a problem since the acetaldehyde is just a quickly passing stage in the digestive process. So far everything is normal. (But you just know there is a fly in the ointment somewhere here, don't you?)

Here we go! Some small amount of the acetaldehyde reacts with a substance in the brain called dopamine. Dopamine is a normal neurotransmitter found in everyone. In fact, without it, we would not be living, breathing entities. The kicker here is that this last bit of biochemistry only happens in alcoholics. The new chemical is (you guessed it) THIQ. This is the same THIQ that was found to be so addictive that it was banned from use in medicine during WWII, even though it is a great painkiller; it's found in heroin addicts and now shows up in the brains of alcoholics as demonstrated by the street people from Texas. So the question arises as to what THIQ does in the brain.

Simply put, it attaches itself to certain receptor sites that don't let go. It is there for keeps and can be found in alcoholics that have been sober for years. It's like the pieces in a jigsaw puzzle that interlock and won't fall out by themselves. We know from experience that sober alcoholics who go back to drinking, even many years later, very quickly find themselves back at the point where they were when they quit. It's not like starting over and gradually working up to the trouble stages, but it's more like one never stopped drinking in the first place. In a period of as little as thirty days, the alcoholics can find themselves back where they were when they quit alcohol years earlier.

WHAT ABOUT THE RATS?

I didn't miss the rat race, but I did kinda miss the rats.
Jerry Nachman[11]

And now it is time to grab the rat by the tail. More than a few alcoholics in rehab have been fortunate enough to watch a film, *The Disease Concept of Alcoholism*, with Dr. David Ohms as the presenter. He presented much of this same information and made perhaps his strongest point talking about the rats. So here is their tale.

A group of rats was bred to have a great dislike for alcohol. In fact, they would rather suffer dehydration rather than drink a mild 3% alcohol solution. These rats would make Carrie Nation[12] proud. The WCTU[13] would welcome them with open arms if they weren't such rats! Then, a small amount of THIQ was injected into the brains of these rats. Carrie would have been appalled at the change. They immediately went for the 80-proof stuff and became instant alcoholics. This was enough to convince most observers (and skeptics) that there is a chemical/organic basis for alcohol addiction. And that is the tale of the rat.

NIGHT SCHOOL

An elderly man is stopped by the police around one a. m. and is asked where he is going at this time of night.

The man replies, "I am going to a lecture about alcohol abuse and the effects it has on the human body."

The officer then asks, "Really? Who is giving that lecture at this time of night?" The man replies, "My wife."

---

[11] Jerry Nachman (1964–2004), vice president, editor-in-chief, MSNBC.
[12] Carrie Nation (1846–1911), crusader against alcohol, would enter saloons and break bottles and fixtures with a hatchet, was often accompanied by hymn-singing women. She was jailed numerous times.
[13] WCTU (Women's Christian Temperance Union), founded in 1847 to combat the influence of alcohol in families and society, also interested in social reform, including labor, prostitution, public health, and sanitation.

The Disease Nature of Alcoholism

Knowledge is power.
Albert Einstein? Not really, at least he didn't say it first.

Knowledge itself is power.
Sir Francis Bacon

There is no knowledge that is not power.
Ralph Waldo Emerson

～

In 2003, an announcement was made that the gene responsible for alcoholism had been isolated (or discovered, if you wish). It was not long before the discovery was challenged. To those who have been told, and have come to believe, that alcoholism is a disease, this is a strange statement. It is time to take a long look at the problem from a historical and scientific perspective and put the issue to rest, at least for our own purposes. We do not expect this will change any minds that have already been made up but rather that it will give support to the idea that addiction to alcohol and many other addictions can be seen as kinds of diseases. It should also be mentioned that the discovery of a gene responsible for alcoholism seems to be a little bit inaccurate and that more recent research indicates that the combination of several genes affects an alcoholic's future.

The word "behaviorist" will be used here to describe a person who believes alcoholism is a result of learned behavior, not a disease.

Let us start with the history of this subject, which would lead one to believe that the behaviorists are correct. Think of the silly things people do under the influence. Cartoons have a wonderful way of expressing the activities of the drunk and showing their funniest actions. We've all seen cartoons depicting intoxicated people who have lampshades on their heads or who are trying to hit on the bosses' spouses at Christmas parties. Real funny in real life, yes? How about the cute pictures with the ice bags on their heads the next morning? For some reason, women seem to duck most of the cartoon fun except as the poor suffering spouses in the background.

Cartoonists fail to deal with the real issues of alcoholic drinking: lost jobs, lost income, missed school and work, hangovers, car repairs, the cost of DWIs, and all those other "fun" events. So it is that when we think of the drunk, we see behavior that is out of line with the rest of the population's behavior. Is it any wonder, then, that the mental health field and behaviorists took the lead in dealing with a problem that manifests itself as weird and out-of-sync behavior? This would seem to be a reasonable approach to the problem. And it seems even more reasonable if we think of the consumption of alcohol as only a behavior and the results of over imbibing as just bad choices we have made. But to take things just a little further, consider this:

If we know someone who was hit in the head by a baseball bat, has some brain damage, and consequently, his or her behavior changes, we say it is not a matter of bad behavior, but rather that it is a physical problem brought about by the injury. Or, we can say the same thing about someone hurt in a car or motorcycle accident when his or her behavior patterns change after a head injury. We are also aware that some external substances can do internal damage to our body systems. Acids or poisons can do permanent damage. Anything that our body cannot tolerate can cause physical damage that can be either short lived (like the poison from a mosquito bite) or permanent, like an acid scar.

So what is a disease? Some dictionaries define it as anything that interferes with normal living. Under this definition, a broken leg is just as much of a disease as the common cold. However, the medical profession adds some more specific qualifications to this definition, such as that it has a group of symptoms. (In the 1960s, Dr. E. M. Jellinek identified over one hundred symptoms and three stages of the development of alcoholism. More on this later.) The medical profession also wants a prognosis of the illness. Does it cure itself, like the common cold, or is it progressive, like untreated cancer? Will it respond to certain treatment and go into remission or become cured? Alcoholism, left untreated, is progressive and will continue to get worse until death—unless something is done. Is there treatment? Yes. Although it is not always successful, it often is. The biggest tragedy here is that it is frequently not treated at all. Has this disease an outcome? Yes, and often it is an untimely death, frequently a violent one. Is there a cause for this disease? For the common cold, it is a virus. For diabetes, there are several factors that encourage its development. Family history is one, along with being overweight, the lack of exercise, and others. And what about alcoholism? Disease or behavior? This is what we attempt to answer as we discuss what is often called the "disease concept" but to us might be more accurately termed the "disease nature" of alcoholism.

Let's take a step back and see where the behaviorists are coming from. It has been pretty well established that some behaviors are learned, often from our parents. For example, parents who severely beat their children usually were subjected to the same treatment when they were growing up. They learned from their parents (by example) that this was the way to bring up children. Without any other model, they believe this must be OK because they believe that they turned out OK. To the behaviorists, this is learned behavior that may be treatable with education. But what about the situation where mom or dad or both use alcohol excessively when stressful situations arise? Some will learn that this is a great way to deal with everyday problems and will take this lesson into adulthood. Is this the root of alcohol abuse and alcoholism? If this were the whole story, then the behaviorists would be right, and alcoholism would be just a choice people made based on their past learning experiences. In some cases, this theory does apply. There is a large group of people who abuse alcohol but are not addicted to its use. One huge group is young adult, college-age drinkers, who abuse themselves with heavy alcohol use until about age 25 or so and then seem to mature and become social drinkers. Excessive use of alcohol is considered one of the rites of adulthood for many of us. The insurance industry has known this for years, as is demonstrated by the significantly higher rates for youth auto insurance. Some people, however, never stop or slow down their drinking, and eventually become full-blown alcoholics. At this point, it would seem that the behavior experts have a very valid argument. A few—very few—people thought there might be more to it.

Way back when the American colonies were thinking of independence from England, there was a doctor named Benjamin Rush. He held some strong opinions, as evidenced by his willingness to sign the Declaration of Independence while knowing his life could be forfeited if the colonists lost the war. He was also a strong advocate for the idea that alcoholism is a disease. Indeed, he was a pioneer in advocating this concept.[14]

However, someone believing and advocating an idea is not proof that the idea is correct. At one time even the most knowledgeable were convinced the world was flat. Carl Jung[15] was a student of the famed Sigmund Freud. While he questioned much of what he learned at Sigmund's knee, he did treat many patients for psychological and behavioral problems. When asked how many alcoholics he had cured, Jung mentioned that just a couple had been cured and that their recoveries seemed to have nothing to do with him; rather, they had had a spiritual experience that seemed to cure them. While this, too, proves nothing, it again suggests something more than just re-learning behavior. Most of Jung's alcoholic patients continued to drink despite his learned treatments, and some other mechanism seemed to affect the recovery of the few that got well.

So does it matter that we think of alcoholism as a disease? We will visit this in the next chapter.

So live that, when you get up in the morning, the Devil says, "Oh crap! She's up and running."

I used to eat a lot of natural foods until I learned that most people die of natural causes.

Garden rule: when weeding, the best way to make sure you are removing a weed and not a valuable plant is to pull on it. If it comes out of the ground easily, it is a valuable plant.

The easiest way to find something that was lost around the house is to buy a replacement.

Never take life seriously. Nobody gets out alive anyway.

Have you noticed that since everyone has a camcorder these days, no one talks about seeing UFOs like they used to?

---

[14] Benjamin Rush (1746–1813), physician, writer, humanitarian, often called the father of American psychiatry.
[15] Carl Gustav Jung (1875–1961), Swiss psychiatrist, founder of analytic psychology.

Alcoholism:
Disease or Behavior?
Does It Matter?

God helps those who don't interfere with His work.
Heard around Al-Anon
~

A while back, some people in recovery were asking whether or not it matters if alcoholism is a disease or a behavior. Fred, with sixteen years sobriety, gave a negative answer. He said, "Whichever it is isn't important. I know what I have to do: don't pick up a drink and go to meetings." This works for him.

Others feel more like Alan, who says the most important thing he learned in rehab was that he had a disease. To him, this made all the difference. He no longer needed to think of himself as a bad person because of his bad behavior. He knew he had behaved badly because of his disease. And his job in recovery was to fix that by making amends and treating the disease that led to the unacceptable behavior.

ALCOHOLISM CAN BE AN EXCUSE

For some—like the parolees mentioned previously—the disease idea is merely an excuse, an excuse to be invoked when facing the parole board, something on the order of "the Devil made me do it, so I'm not responsible." What they overlook is that, as people generally learn in rehab, you are not responsible for having a

27

disease. But now that you know this, you ARE responsible for your recovery!

HOW ABOUT THE CO-DEPENDENTS?

We have mentioned the alcoholics. What about those who live with them, work with them, and may be surrounded by them? Does it matter to us whether or not the alcoholic has a bona fide disease?

Here is what one woman said, in reference to her alcoholic parents, who are now dead. "I grew up feeling so unloved because my parents weren't there for me. As I have learned about the disease nature of alcoholism, I now realize I was totally loved."

Understanding the disease factor of alcoholism has made a profound difference to her because it means the difference between feeling loved or unloved. She realized that the behavior of the alcoholics was a result of the drink, not a lack of caring. Her parents were unable to show how much they cared because the disease had robbed them of the ability to be nurturing parents. This is a common feeling among children of alcoholics.

I MAY HAVE CHOOSEN TO HAVE A DRINK,
BUT I NEVER CHOSE TO BECOME AN ALCOHOLIC

Some people have observed that alcoholism is not a fault but that alcoholics are unwilling victims of this disease. This could just as well be said of us who live with them. Of course, we may choose to end an alcoholic relationship, making our life lovely from then on, right? Ask those who have tried it. Most will tell you that, without treatment for themselves, they began another relationship with an alcoholic—or some other less-than-sane person.

Knowing a loved one has a disease and that we are affected by it gives us a certain power—if nothing else, it gives us the ability to see what is really going on. People experiencing heart disease, the aftermath of a stroke, or even a broken leg often act abnormally and sometimes behave badly. Does knowing they are sick make it is easier to live with people whose behavior is hurtful or embarrassing? Some have compared alcoholism with Alzheimer's disease; sick people often behave in a crazy way. Talk to anyone who cares for such a patient about the frustration of life with someone who gets out of the house and runs the streets naked, cussing the passersby. Or burns the important mail. Or lashes out at the caregivers, sometimes causing bodily harm.

Laugh insanely, love truly, and forgive quickly.
Unknown

28

FAMILY DYSFUNCTION

Whenever one member of a family group has a major disease, it leads to a somewhat dysfunctional family. If one member, such a crippled elderly parent or grandparent, requires a disproportionate amount of the family's time, it puts stress on the other members, which results in some degree of dysfunction. In general the severity of the problem is related to the amount of attention required by the ill member of the family. And sometimes, they can be far more demanding than an alcoholic or addict.

ANOTHER KIND OF DYSFUNCTION

Living with sick people is not easy under any conditions. A recent study of elder abuse found that the sicker the patient, the worse the abuse. And the spouse is often the abuser. Are these abusive people horrible creatures? Not really. They are probably average human beings who are in a situation causing them to be long on frustration and short on patience. Not a lot different from those of us living with alcoholics. We are often inclined to use weapons of sarcasm and unkindness on our alcoholic family members. It is easier for us and more conducive to family harmony to accept what we cannot change and build on the good that is there.

DRAWING LINES OR SETTING BOUNDARIES

Should we learn to accept dangerous, unacceptable behavior? No. We must protect ourselves and the family members for whom we are responsible. A case comes to mind of a devoted husband and father who began acting more and more irrational and even dangerous. It turned out he was not into drugs but that he had a fast-growing brain tumor. Of course, this was not his fault and he loved his family dearly, as they loved him. However, for their own safely, it was necessary for them to remove themselves from the situation.

Recognizing that we are dealing with a disease and being aware of its symptoms makes life more manageable in the sense that we do not set ourselves up for disappointment and can become more realistic about our loved one's illness. We become more accepting of reality and more able to make personal changes that can help us have a more serene and useful life. We learn to accept what we cannot change and to change what we can.

WHAT IS ADDICTION?

When we wanted to know the meaning of a word, our teachers told us to look it up in the dictionary. Here are a couple of definitions:

From Webster's Imperial Dictionary of 1909 comes our official definition: addiction (n.), the act of devoting or giving up to in practice, the state of being devoted.

A newer definition is from Random House in 1997: addiction (n.), the state of being enslaved to a habit or practice or to something that is psychologically or physically habit-forming, as narcotics, to such an extent that its cessation causes severe trauma.

An addict might call it a descent into hell.

> **I am fighting for my life against this**
> **thing that would destroy me.**
> **Sue, an alcohol/heroin addict, after multiple times in rehab**

Here is a good working definition from Len: any compulsive or habitual excessive behavior or substance use that causes problems in your life, e.g., problems with work, school, family relations, friendships, parenting, finances, or legal problems.

One of the best descriptions of addiction is that of a swimmer who stays close to the surface because he must breathe air. If he is caught in weeds or tide and pulled down, he knows he will die if he tries to breathe and holds out as long as he can. But, eventually he has to take that breath, his lungs fill with water, and he dies. Why do people choose to become addicted? They don't; they just want to swim and don't believe they will be pulled under. There are many addictions, some to chemicals, some to behaviors, but they all work in the same way. Not everybody knows this.

For quite a few years, my neighbor down the street and I were close. Our kids played together, we borrowed the cup of sugar or two eggs from each other, sometimes gave each other rides. We knew each other quite well. Or did we?

One lovely spring morning, I was standing in my driveway when this neighbor came by. I said, "Hi, how are you?" Her mouth opened. Rage and anguish came spewing out like a stream of toxic waste. She spoke of her husband's compulsive gambling and how it was ruining their family. I knew things weren't quite right in their house and had some ideas but was too wrapped up in my own misery to pay much attention. She finished ranting, continued walking up the street, and never mentioned it again.

I was beyond dumbfounded. I could only stand in the driveway muttering to myself, "Compulsive gambler. Compulsive drinker. Compulsive drinker. Compulsive gambler.

Of the two, I'll take the compulsive drinker." Years later, when I learned all addictions had the same basis, I was surprised—but not very. It made sense.

Daffy

The twenty-first century has brought with it a plethora of addictions, some of which have been made easier by the Internet. Others exist because of the Internet. Pornography has probably always been with us. Maybe cave dwellers carved dirty pictures on the smoky back walls of the cave, but the Internet has made it accessible to all. More than one employee has been fired for indulging a porn addiction on company time. Excessive shopping is another addiction enhanced by the 'Net, which, despite the jokes, can be harmful to a family when it takes money away from necessities. Also, the use of email, Facebook, Twitter, fantasy football, etc., can easily become addictions that steal personal time as well as work time from your employer.

It is common to see young people overindulging in video games and TV. Childhood obesity is a problem of national proportions. When we look back at class pictures from our youth, we see perhaps one fairly overweight kid in our class. We were too busy riding our bikes, playing hide-and-seek, and running around to let the pounds build up. But it's not just youth who have this problem. Many adults sit glued to the tube that gives them escape from their painful or mundane lives.

Some of us co-dependents have thought it would be wonderful to have a spouse addicted to work instead of chemicals. But for those who have been there and done that, it is quite otherwise. Work can be an escape as much as booze, although it is a more socially acceptable addiction. It can rob a family of the attention of a parent or a spouse and cause serious family problems.

Food addiction doesn't sound like much. People in Overeaters Anonymous sometimes say: "The alcoholic can lock his tiger in a cage and walk away. The overeater has to take his tiger out and walk it three times a day." Anorexia and bulimia have been the cause of death for some, and these addictions almost always cause family disruption. One woman had to keep food locked in the trunk of her car because her daughter would eat anything and everything in the house. One grossly overweight diabetic had stomach-shrinking surgery and was doing well eating the smaller amounts prescribed. But the lure of food was too strong and the patient began trying to eat again as insanely as before, effectively stretching the stomach toward its previous capacity. Does this not meet the description of being pulled under by the addiction?

What is going on here? It's much more complex than this, but put simply, there is a "pleasure center" in the human brain. There are also neurotransmitters that activate neurons, which eventually affect the brain's pleasure center. Behaviors or substances both work in a similar manner. For instance, smoking, which is legal and has not always been considered a serious addiction, gives to the average pack-and-a-half-a-day smoker about 300 small highs each day. Is it any wonder that addiction to nicotine (the addictive drug in cigarettes) is so hard to break?

There are things that can be done, but none of them are easy. People recovering from addiction will tell you it is worth it. Imagine the freedom an ex-smoker feels when finally she doesn't need to go out at 11:30 p.m. to buy cigarettes to be sure she has one when she wakes up in the morning.

So, we can see that whether addiction is a disease or a behavior, it always causes massive problems for the addicted one and for that person's loved ones.

◁☺▷
TWO BOYS

The story goes that some psychologists were studying a couple of little boys, one a joyful optimist, one a mournful pessimist. They placed the pessimist in Room A, full of wonderful toys of all kinds. The optimist was put in Room B, full of manure. A couple of hours later, they went to check out the situation. Piteous wails were coming from Room A. They found the boy sitting on the floor crying his eyes out.

"Why, whatever is wrong? Don't you like the toys?"

"It's not that," came the answer, "but with all these toys, I'm sure to break one." From Room B came the sound of happy whistling. Entering, they saw the lad shoveling and shoveling.

"What's going on?" They said. Without missing a beat, the young man cheerfully exclaimed,

"Well, with all this poop, there's gotta be a pony in here somewhere!"

Who Put the Dope in My Dopamine?

Stop acting like such a dope!
One kid to another

~

As youngsters, we heard about "dope," which was some kind of bad stuff that some people used. It was far away from most of our young minds, and when we wondered about dope, we guessed that the people who used it were dopes and acted dopey or were all doped up. It was also the stuff we used to glue model airplanes together, and sniffing it made us feel funny, perhaps even a little dopey ourselves. It seemed like a good idea to not breathe it in. Most of us had never heard of dopamine. This is what we learn from an etymology dictionary about the word *dope*: it is American English, meaning "sauce, gravy," from Dutch *doop*, "thick dipping sauce." The definition continues: the extension to "drug" begins in 1889 from the practice of smoking semi-liquid opium preparation. The meaning of *dope* as a "foolish, stupid person" is older (1851) and may have a sense of "thick-headed." The sense of "inside information" (1901) may come from knowing before the race which horse had been drugged to influence performance. *Dope-fiend* is attested from 1896.

And that has nothing to do with airplane glue.

Let's take a quick look at dopamine and a few other related things:

Dopamine is a neurotransmitter that we all have in our bodies. Without it we die. With abnormal amounts, either too much or too little, we get sick. Perhaps the best-known neurotransmitter is adrenaline, the fight-or-flight transmitter that we have all experienced at one time or another in a time of great or sudden stress or danger.

Neurotransmitters are chemicals that act between neurons (nerve cells) to make them active. Receptor sites are areas where neurotransmitters attach to neurons to cause cells to activate.

Neurons are nerve cells that let us know all kinds of things, like when we have a toothache, what our eyes see, what the smooth skin of a baby feels like, how much that stubbed toe hurts, etc. We have a pretty good idea of what nerves do and that they are the main information system throughout the body, and many are concentrated in the spinal column and the brain. Some nerve cells are very long and carry "messages" long distances.

Synapse is the name that is given to the spaces between the neurons, and this is where the neurotransmitters do their work. Dopamine and the other neurotransmitters allow one neuron to "fire," or relay information, to the next one in line to keep the chain going on up to and inside the brain.

Agonists are chemicals that help or enhance the action of a substance—in this case, dopamine. Some examples are nicotine, muscarine (from the muscana mushroom), and a-latroxine (which is released by the black widow spider bite).

Antagonists, on the other hand, have just the opposite effect. They hinder and interfere with the action, in this case, of the dopamine. Examples here are curare (poison), botulinus toxin, and atropine.

A great deal of research has now been done on dopamine, and some very interesting discoveries have come to light. Many mood-altering drugs alter the dopamine balance. In the pleasure center of the brain, an excess of dopamine will have the pleasure cells firing more frequently, giving the feeling of great well-being. Some well-known diseases are associated with the production—or lack of production—of dopamine. Parkinson's disease is treated with a drug called L-dopa, which can be changed into dopamine in the brain to help make up for a loss of natural dopamine production. The onset of Alzheimer's disease is also delayed in some individuals who use drugs that increase dopamine availability in the cranium. Schizophrenia is another condition that seems to be associated with an unbalanced dopamine level. In this case it appears that an overproduction of dopamine is the villain, and drugs that retard the production of dopamine seem to help the victims.

Like we mentioned earlier, nicotine, the addicting drug found in tobacco, has the ability to stimulate the pleasure center of the brain (via increased dopamine action) about 300 times a day for a smoker who consumes about a pack and a half of cigarettes a day. Just think about it—300 little pleasure hits a day!

Now, exactly how do these drugs work in connection with the dopamine? It would take a full PhD dissertation to cover all that is known and speculated on this subject, so let's just talk briefly about two common drugs and how they affect the neurotransmitter picture.

Cocaine and amphetamine are two commonly abused drugs. They both cause an increase in dopamine in the synapse, resulting in more activity in the receptor neuron and causing more activity in the pleasure center of the brain. But each does it in a different way. Cocaine works by stopping the uptake of dopamine (normally done by antagonists) and thus makes more dopamine available in the synapse. Amphetamine, on the other hand, helps release more dopamine from the cells into the synapse. So now we have two drugs that have the same effect—providing more dopamine—but that work in different ways and MIGHT need to be treated differently in cases of addiction.

This is an oversimplification of a very complex subject. It is hard to know how much information to give. While there's such a thing as too much information, we also know that too little knowledge is a dangerous thing. But does it really matter to us? This is interesting, perhaps, but we know what WE need to do. We are responsible for our own recovery. Let's work on that!

◁☺▷

If the government was really serious about preventing people from drinking,
then driving, they wouldn't allow bars to have parking lots.
Letter to a local newspaper

The Worst Drug of All!

If we wonder often, the gift of knowledge will come.
Arapaho Proverb

~

Which IS the worst drug of all? What do you think?

Some drugs are considered "gateway" drugs. They are often the first ones that people use, and they often lead to the use of more and stronger drugs. In our kitchens, bathrooms, offices, and even the kids' rooms, we can often find items that are categorized as "inhalants." Some of the things that kids sniff to get high include magic markers, correcting fluid, gasoline, and almost any solvent. You get the idea. One of the scariest things about inhalants is that they can cause heart failure on the very first use. And they are gateway drugs that may lead to more potent drugs later. These inhalants are often the first drugs tried by the very young. And if your child is one of the rare ones who dies from that first use, inhalants are the worst thing you can imagine and are the gateway to your nightmares.

Inhalants are not the only gateway drugs. There are many more that are often the kickoff to further drug use. When asked, most people think of marijuana as a good candidate. And they are right: it is one of the gateway drugs. It is illegal from the start, so progression to another illegal drug is a minor change in the minds of many users. Another factor is that pot is not considered to be physically addicting. There is growing evidence, however, that it is psychologically addicting. But its main claim to the "most dangerous" title is that it is one of the gateway drugs.

Not all the "gateway" drugs—or for that matter, the most dangerous ones—are illegal. One claimant to the "most dangerous" title is alcohol. But you know, it's legal if you are over 21, and it is used all the time in social situations, often to celebrate. And sometimes it's used to drown your sorrows or just to pass the time of day. With that, we are looking at someone who drinks to excess and is probably an alcoholic. We all know of the wonderful things alcohol can do, like kill germs, sterilize the toilet, and dissolve medicines to make them easier to take...as well as kill you, sterilize a relationship, and dissolve marriages. Sometimes it acts as a lubricant, as in it lubricates the brain until it slides right out from under its owner. And perhaps it also lubricates the road so that accidents happen. At any rate, it is one of the most used (and abused) drugs around. Could this be our worst drug? It is estimated that about 10% of the population is alcoholic or has the predisposition for alcoholism. That's a lot of people. And perhaps 70% of the population drinks. Sometimes even social drinkers get excessive in their consumption, and, not being accustomed to the effects of heavy drinking, they are less able to handle themselves than alcoholics under the same influence. Yes, a case can be made for alcohol being our most evil drug.

In addition to alcohol, there is another legal drug. What about the use of tobacco? Could that be the worst drug? Nicotine is extremely addictive and if not already legal, should never have been allowed on the open market. The main problem is that, for a long time, we didn't have scientific proof of the devastating effects of the over 2,000 chemicals found in tobacco smoke. We have suspected it for years, and even in the early 1900s, cigarettes were often called "cancer sticks" and "coffin nails." Tobacco was introduced into Europe (by some of Columbus's sailors) in the late 1490s, and by the early 1500s there was already suspicion that tobacco was a cause of some cancers.

Almost one-third of our population smokes. It is estimated that a smoker's life is shortened by seven to fourteen years. The U.S., all its high-tech medicine notwithstanding, only ranks 27th in world life expectancy rates. Poor diet and lack of exercise can account for some of it. But averaging in the shorter life spans of smokers does contribute to our low ranking. (And we haven't even mentioned all the work and productivity lost to sick time. Did we say that the jump from tobacco to stronger drugs also puts it into the gateway class? Smoking tobacco and jumping to pot is a small hop for many.)

No other drug can do so much to destroy the human body and making it age and uglify quite as rapidly and completely as methamphetamine. There are Internet sites showing the before and after pictures of meth users that are totally amazing—and gross. In just a few months, meth addicts age years, and their teeth and gums deteriorate remarkably.

We could go on and make a case for every class of mind-altering drugs. However, an addicted person and that person's family members will be most influenced by the evils of the addicted person's drug of choice. How much someone else suffers over any particular chemical means nothing next to that one that is tearing down your life.

Here is the story of Mrs. Jones, and we have all met Mrs. Jones and her sisters in some form:

> Mrs. Jones was a teacher, and she was a very good one. She had a way about her that meant business but let her students know she really cared about them. At a staff meeting one day, the danger of drugs was being discussed and heroin had top billing.

> Mrs. Jones very forcefully said, "Heroin never gave me one sleepless night. Alcohol has given me many!" Her husband was an alcoholic whom she divorced after 20 years of marriage. He finally died of alcoholism. So, for Mrs. Jones, alcohol was the worst drug. Or was it? She was a dedicated smoker who considered it her divine right to smoke and was incensed when smoking was banned in the school building.

> Just before Christmas vacation one year, Mrs. Jones came in sporting an oxygen tank, which she had to carry up and down the stairs. She said her doctor told her she would could either stop smoking or die. She really tried, but the addiction was too powerful and she was too far gone. Shortly before Easter vacation, she had a stroke and died, depriving the students of a fine teacher who could have given her unique gifts to another generation of children.

THE WORST DRUG IS THE ONE THAT IS GIVING YOU THE MOST TROUBLE.

◁☺▷
AN APPLE FOR THE TEACHER?

On the first day of school, the children brought gifts for their teacher.

The florist's son brought the teacher a big bouquet of roses.

The candy-store owner's daughter gave the teacher a delicious bag of salt-water taffy from Coney Island.

The baker's twins brought a beautifully decorated chocolate cake.

Then the liquor store owner's son brought up a big, heavy box. The teacher lifted it up and noticed that it was leaking a little.

She touched a drop of the liquid with her finger and tasted it. Is it wine?" she guessed.

"No," the boy replied. She tasted another drop and asked, "Champagne?"

"No," said the little boy, "It's a puppy!"

Who'd a Thunk It? A Few Observations

Things are not always what they seem.
Phaedrus[16]

DRY OR SOBER

Now and then around recovering people you might hear that an alcoholic is dry but not sober. Aren't dry and sober the same? Not exactly. A dry alcoholic is not drinking. A sober one is developing the serenity to be "comfortable in his or her own skin." A sober alcoholic is a joy to be around, but a dry one is not so. As you are with the wet ones, with dry alcoholics you are always waiting for the other shoe to drop.

Often a person has had an ultimatum from an outside source. The doctor says, "Your whiskey or your life." Or the judge says, "Your whiskey or your liberty." Some diehards choose to drink themselves to death or risk hard time in prison. Most people prefer to try abstinence. Some immediately seek out a 12-Step program and take the first shaky step on the long journey to sobriety and serenity. Others just give up the booze. For them it's a hard road. They are "white-knuckling" it all the way.

One educator stopped drinking with no plan but to not drink. Good start, but it was not enough. He became a maniac with unbridled nervous energy. His colleagues—and probably his family— often wished he'd go back to drinking. Finally he went to a good alcohol counselor who worked with him, getting him to slow down,

---

[16] Phaedrus (15 BC–AD 50), Roman fabulist.

minimize stress, and live in the present—one day at a time. Some recovering friends met him a few years later and observed that he was a different person, calm and serene. He said, "Now I know what you meant. For three years I was dry. Now I am sober." Incidentally, he said his co-workers' lack of understanding was one of the hardest things for him. They couldn't see how he could be an alcoholic when he wasn't drinking.

CHANGING ADDICTIONS

"Frank has quit drinking and we will live happily ever after."

"Happily ever after" is where the frog turns into a prince, where little girls and little pigs triumph over the wicked wolf, and where a kiss brings the princess out of a hundred-year coma. Not the same as the world of utility payments, auto breakdowns, calls from irate teachers, work deadlines—you know the world.

Sometimes, maybe not often, but sometimes, the door closes on one addiction and opens on another. A heroin addict becomes an alcoholic. An alcoholic may turn to food or pot or sex to fill the void. We know of one alcoholic who was in recovery from his alcohol addiction and was doing well at that. But he had also had cancer of the throat and received surgery for it. He was an avid smoker, and even though he had a tracheotomy and had to talk with a mechanical device, he continued smoking—through his tracheotomy. His smoking had increased with the loss of his alcohol.

What to do? The advice given to folks coming into AA is simple: don't pick up a drink, but come to meetings and your life will get better. The same goes for any addiction. There are groups for gamblers, drug addicts, sex addicts, food addicts, etc., although the meetings are fewer and farther between. Whatever the addiction, AA can help. There are a few old-timers who feel Alcoholics Anonymous is just for alcoholics, but they are rapidly becoming outnumbered. Counseling is good too, especially if the counselor is familiar with addiction. Above all, realize that this is another addiction that needs to be dealt with.

What about us, the co-dependents, so elated at the end of one addiction and so deflated by the beginning of another? What do you think? Al-Anon is still there. Get back to it, get to extra meetings, make phone calls to members who have had useful things to say or have dealt with this in the past. As they are for people with addictions, counselors can be very useful in this situation.

Above all, don't give up on yourself!!!

◁☺▷
SENIOR MOMENT

A senior citizen said to his eighty-year old buddy:

"So I hear you're getting married?"

"Yep!"

"Do I know her?"

"Nope!"

"This woman, is she good looking?"

"Not really."

"Is she a good cook?"

"Naw, she can't cook too well."

"Does she have lots of money?"

"Nope! Poor as a church mouse."

"Well, then, is she good in bed?"

"I don't know."

"Why in the world do you want to marry her then?"

"Because she can still drive!"

How 'Bout
Some History?

What has been will be again.
What has been done will be done again.
There is nothing new under the sun.
Ecclesiastes 1:9

~

Have we seen enough heavy stuff for a while? We have been told we must get rid of beliefs and behaviors that have been building for years, sometimes for our entire lifetimes. Old ideas die hard and change takes time. Would you like to take a break? Think of this chapter as the teacher letting you out of class early with no new homework.

There's an epitaph from a grave in ancient Egypt that refers to the occupant having enjoyed the grapes too much. But we also know that even the ancient Egyptians had some medicines. It is safe to assume that if they had experimented and had some herbs that were beneficial, they had also come across some of the not so beneficial ones. Some, by the odds, must have made them feel good. And that is the reason people use drugs today—to feel good. We don't know just when someone first licked a certain species of frog and got high from its skin secretions (ugh), but that person may have felt like he or she had found Prince Charming. What do you suppose prompted someone to lick that frog? That aside, we can safely assume that mind-altering drugs (including alcohol, of course) have been with us for a long, long time. And the markings on that ancient grave tell us that they have also been a problem for a long, long time.

As we have previously mentioned, one of the signers of the *Declaration of Independence* back in 1776 was a Doctor Benjamin Rush. Besides being a patriot willing to put his signature on a document that could have cost him dearly had the Revolutionary War not come out favorably for the rebels, he also was an early advocate of alcoholism as a disease rather than a behavioral no-no. He was a pioneer in this belief and unfortunately, his views died with him.

Women's lives have long been made difficult by drunken husbands. In the 1800s a temperance movement sprang up in the U.S. The definition of temperance has to do with moderation. But this movement wanted to put an end to the sale of liquor. While Susan B. Anthony and Elizabeth Cady Stanton were working on the suffrage movement to get women the right to vote, Carrie Nation of the temperance movement was working to get rid of the saloons. Nation chopped her way into history by breaking up saloons with her little hatchet.

For most of recorded history, people have been making and ingesting ethanol, the drinkable form of alcohol. Most other forms are more poisonous to the human body and will make us physically ill, and some are toxic enough to kill even in fairly small amounts. While there are few around that remember Prohibition, many of us have heard the tales of "bathtub gin" and how some "wood alcohol" was produced by accident (or lack of knowledge) and made some people blind and poisoned others. People took many chances in those days to get their booze. Gangsters like Al Capone were welcome in high society as folk heroes in those days. Man wanted his feel-good pacifier, and so Prohibition went the way of the horse and buggy.

Remember that Freud, toward the end of his life, stated that all behavioral illnesses would someday be shown to have a biochemical origin. A huge amount of evidence is piled up that supports this concept for the disease of alcoholism. As we know today, most "mental diseases" are being treated with drugs, which are often chemicals that work on the symptoms of the mental illness.

It might seem that alcoholism should be treated by the medical community rather than the mental health field. But when we consider that most of the symptoms are behavior related (the lampshade-on-the-head kind of thing), it is understandable that the field of mental health took over. Even today, the average medical student only gets a few hours of training in alcoholism. There's a (not-so-funny) joke that medical students have the 4-2-1 training in alcoholism: 4 years of medical school with 2 hours devoted to our number 1 health problem. Yet the effects of alcohol on the human body put many patients in the hands of medical doctors. They come to doctors for injuries resulting from being intoxicated or because of long-term illnesses like cirrhosis of the liver. Since many doctors see these problems as preventable, and since they have minimal schooling in the disease, it is not too surprising that many of them still think of alcoholism as a behavioral problem. A recent poll shows that while the population as a whole now believes alcoholism to be a disease, less than half of MDs believe it—even though the AMA pronounced it a disease in the mid-1950s!

In the 1960s Dr. E. M. Jellinek published his work on "The Disease Concept of Alcoholism." In this work, he showed the progress of alcoholism from its beginning to the final conclusion, which is usually death if the disease is not arrested. He listed over one hundred symptoms and broke the progression of an alcoholic into three stages. In the first stage he noted that the symptoms are easily disguised and not recognized. They are easiest to treat in this early stage, but like so many diseases, the early symptoms are lighter and often ignored. The middle stages allow for much easier recognition and also include the beginnings of physical problems. By the late stages, everyone knows that someone is an alcoholic and treatment is the most difficult. Many do not even live long enough to reach this stage.

So we have a disease from which very few recovered. Having this disease was considered a sin, a lack of willpower, a lack of common sense, and a comical problem. By this same token, if you know anyone who has smoked and tried to quit, ask him or her about addiction and the physical craving for nicotine. And are they people who are behaving badly? Since they represent over 20% of US citizens, we hope not.

The entertainment industry has quite an effect on popular thinking about alcoholism. From the beginning, in the movies drunkenness was portrayed as a comical thing. Fans of old movies can point to characters played by Charlie Chaplin, W. C. Fields, and others. But that's not the whole story. There have been some sober (pun intended) acknowledgments of the seriousness of the problem. There were *The Lost Weekend, Smash-Up—the Story of a Woman, Days of Wine and Roses, Come, Fill the Cup*, and others. The year 1952 saw the first extensive introduction to AA in the way of 12-Step calls, meetings, slogans, prayers, etc., with "Come Back Little Sheba" and "Something to Live For." The experience of a woman in rehab was shown in *28 Days*. In the '60s, there began to be a shift from portraying alcohol abuse to excesses in other drugs.

One of the popular films portraying an alcoholic was *Arthur*, the tale of an alcoholic who finds true love, marries, and lives happily ever after without alcohol. Not so. This is never-never land at its finest. How many folks do you know who have been cured of cancer—or diabetes, or any disease—by finding true love?

Many decades ago, a popular play was based on the disease. It was called *The Drunkard* and was exactly what the title suggests. Theatergoers rolled in the aisles with this one. Recently a little theater group in our area put on *The Drunkard*, causing one of the addiction professionals to remark, "It was funny? I can't wait 'til they do a play on cancer."

Despite popular and often erroneous ideas about alcoholism, in 1935, two men founded AA (Alcoholics Anonymous). They started AA with the premise that alcoholism was a disease, and since then many alcoholics have been getting better. This story and the spin-off of Al-Anon will come later. The history of how some alcoholics started getting well will also come later. In the meantime, remember, only you can make it a great day!

◁☺▷
GOOD DEED

A man appeared before the venerable Saint Peter at the Pearly Gates. "Have you ever done anything of particular merit?" Saint Peter asked the man. "Well, I can think of one thing," the man offered.

"On a trip to the Black Hills of South Dakota, I came upon a gang of bikers who was threatening a young woman. I directed them to leave her alone, but they wouldn't listen. So, I approached the largest and most heavily tattooed biker and smacked him in the face, kicked his bike over, ripped out his nose ring, and threw it on the ground. I yelled, 'Now, back off, or I'll kick the stuffing out of all of you!'"

Saint Peter was impressed. "When did this happen?"

"Couple of minutes ago."

Love Story

Love suffers long...
I Corinthians 13

~

Once—not once upon a time, because this is a true story—there was a tall, handsome soldier named Bill who loved a pretty girl named Lois. She was crazy about him, so they were married just before he left for France to serve as an artillery officer in World War I.

After the war, they settled in New York City, where Bill became a stockbroker. For a while, he traveled the country, checking out various companies for his firm. Often Lois went along, going by car or motorcycle. Lois had a hidden agenda—she was hoping to keep Bill from drinking.

When the market crashed in 1929, more than one fellow jumped from the 27th floor. Bill was not one of these. But he drank more and more.

Both Lois and Bill wanted a family, but Lois had ectopic pregnancies and could never bear children. They tried the adoption route but were turned down. They found out that they were blacklisted due to Bill's excessive drinking.

In 1933, Bill was admitted to the Charles B. Townes Hospital for Alcohol and Drug Addiction, under the care of Dr. William D. Silkworth. Dr. Silkworth was unusual because he believed alcoholism was a matter of both physical and mental control: the manifestation of a physical allergy (the physical inability to stop drinking, once started) and an obsession of the mind (to take the first drink).

Bill gained hope from the doctor's assertion that alcoholism was a medical condition, not a moral failing. Even that hope was insufficient to stop the drinking, however. Bill was told that he would either die of alcoholism or be locked up permanently due to Wernike encephalopathy, commonly known as "wet brain."

In November of 1934, Ebby, an old drinking buddy, showed up. Bill looked forward to boozing it up with his friend. But Ebby was not the same good old boy. He wasn't drinking and told Bill he'd been sober for several weeks under the guidance of the Oxford Group.[17] Bill had some interest in what Ebby said, but not much.

Later he was admitted to Townes Hospital for his fourth and last visit. One night, while lying in bed, depressed and despairing, he cried out, "I'll do anything. Anything at all. If there be a God, let Him show Himself." He then had the sensation of a bright light, a feeling of ecstasy, and a new serenity. He never drank again. He told Dr. Silkworth, who said, "Something has happened to you. I don't understand it, but you had better hang on to it!" Bill joined the Oxford Group and tried to help other alcoholics, without success. But he realized this was enabling him to stay sober.

In 1935, on a business trip to Akron, Ohio, Bill found himself in a hotel lobby that had a bar down the hall. He wanted desperately to walk down and have a drink. He needed help. There was a directory of churches on the wall. Bill went down the list and one call put him in touch with a Dr. Bob, who was in the local chapter of the Oxford Group.

The doc wasn't particularly interested in someone trying to help him, but Bill assured him that he, Bill, was the one who needed help. The men talked for hours and became friends. Good thing, because Dr. Bob was in trouble and close to being barred from the hospital for showing up plastered much of the time. Actually, at one point, Dr. Bob was scheduled to put someone under the knife, but his hands were too shaky. So Bill gave him his last drink to steady his hands for the surgery.

At one point, Bill and Dr. Bob decided they needed another drunk to help. So they went to the hospital and found one. The "helping drunks" talked to him for a while, telling their stories, and said they would be back. Next day, not expecting too much, Bill and Dr. Bob went back. They found the man with his wife, telling her a

---

[17] The Oxford Group, a Christian movement primarily in Europe and America in the 1920s and 1930s, founded by Dr. Frank Buchman, influential in Alcoholics Anonymous—its founders were members until 1940. Bill W. acknowledged "early AA's got ideas of self examination, acknowledgment of character defects, restitution for harm done, working with others, straight from the Oxford Group and Sam Shoemaker, their former leader in America."

story of the two angels who had come to him the night before, angels who understood his problem. He left the hospital, never to drink again. So Bill D. joined Bill W. and Dr. Bob as the third member of the group of sober drunks.

Bill spent the summer in Akron at Dr. Bob's house, where he was treated like a family member. Bob's wife, Anne S., was a generous, kind woman who welcomed everyone into her home and was a great force for good in the new group of men trying to stay sober.

Back home, Bill worked with alcoholics in the Oxford Group, referred to as the "nameless squad of drunks." He often brought them home and Lois welcomed them with a boiling coffee pot.

The men saw a need for some guidelines. Something needed to be written down for this fledgling organization. Bill felt that the principles of the Oxford Group would be useful. But some were turned off by "all that God stuff" and wanted any reference to God left out.

Lois was listening from the kitchen and when Bill came and asked her opinion, she told him basically that it was the power of God that had brought them this far...so they left God in, but they referred to a Higher Power and God as we understand Him. Then they hammered out the 12 Steps. They put together the "BIG BOOK," known as the "AA Bible." Bill believed that anonymity was a key principle, a cornerstone of the fellowship. He felt this so strongly that he refused to have his picture taken for the cover of *Time* magazine—even from the back!

In the late '30s and '40s, people—overwhelmingly men—were meeting in various cities studying the 12 Steps and sharing their "experience, strength, and hope." Often, their wives (and sometimes their children) accompanied them. Friendships were begun; these women had a special bond.

Lois was always having AA fellows in her home and going with Bill to meetings all over the city. She had great love and the patience of a saint. But even a saint can run low on patience. One night, when Bill asked her if she was ready to go to the meeting, Lois screamed, "Damn your old meetings!" and threw a shoe at him. This surprised Bill, but probably not as much as it surprised Lois. This was not totally rational behavior—and she was the sane one? She realized that she needed serenity herself. She talked with some of the other wives and they began to meet for their own sanity and spirituality, using the same 12 Steps that were so helpful to their husbands. Lois W. and Anne B. founded Al-Anon in 1951.

> It only takes one person to start something,
> but many others to carry it out.
> Lois W.

Lois and Bill were homeless many times and stayed at the homes of friends during several years of their marriage. They moved fifty-two times in two years. In 1941, due to an offer from the widow of an alcoholic, they were able to purchase their first home: Stepping Stones, in Katonah, NY, just outside New York City. Stepping Stones is now designated a state and national historic place.

This started out to be about the love story between Lois and Bill, but it has expanded to take in much more love. There's the love of Dr. Bob's wife, Anne S., who was mother to the early AA's of Akron, opening her home and giving them all kinds of support. She also gave encouragement to Lois in the early days of Bill's sobriety. There were the women coming together in New York City and Akron while their husbands were meeting, who leaned on each other's experience, strength, and hope. There was Anne B., the fearful, sickly child who learned to turn to her Higher Power and blossomed into a fearless, competent woman and co-founder of Al-Anon. There are many nameless women—and a few men, but remember, Al-Anon began with women—who kept welcoming newcomers and showing, by their example of selfless service, that there was hope for a better life.

This love continues down to the present.

> When I walked into the meeting, Jeanette greeted me. I saw
> in her eyes a depth of pain that was mine. I knew she
> understood. But that's not all. There was an unconditional
> love that was for me, as well as the others. I knew this is
> where I belonged. I would be back.
> Cindy, Al-Anon member

It's not unusual to have someone come to a meeting, then many more, and just sit and blubber. No one thinks this strange. Many have done it. Then, after a few weeks or months, the person is lighter, even laughing. The situation at home may not have changed, but the person has.

There's a saying in Al-Anon that you—the newcomer—may not like us all, but you will come to love us in a special way, the way we already love you.

Lois and Bill had over half a century together. He died on their 53rd anniversary, at the age of 75. Lois continued the work they had devoted so much of their lives to. At the age of 94 she was the principle speaker at the 55th anniversary convention of Alcoholics Anonymous.

Lois died at 97. A story has it that, on her deathbed, Lois was conscious but unable to speak. A friend reminded her of what a great force for good she had been. Lois pointed upward, as if to say, "It was God." The friend replied, "But you were His instrument." Then Lois pointed to the friend as if to say, "So were you."

From AA came not only Al-Anon, but a host of other groups—Gamblers Anonymous, Narcotics Anonymous, Overeaters Anonymous, and Sex Addicts Anonymous, to name a few. Hundreds of thousands of lives have been changed for the good by these groups.

It's said that there is power in a few dedicated people to change the world. Well, you could count on one hand the people in 1935 who started AA, which became the most positive movement of the 20th century!

Material for this chapter comes from many sources, including:
- Various Al-Anon pamphlets: "Lois's Story," "Anne's Story," "The Co-Founders,"
- Bill W's speech to AA group the day of Dr. Bob's death,
- Stepping Stones, and
- Wikipedia.

If you are interested in Bill and Lois, visit your library or video store and check out *My Name is Bill W.* and *The Lois Wilson Story: When Love is Not Enough.*

◁☺▷
GREAT TRUTHS LITTLE CHILDREN HAVE LEARNED
1. No matter how hard you try, you can't baptize cats.
2. When your Mom is mad at your Dad, don't let her brush your hair.
3. If your sister hits you, don't hit her back. Parents always catch the second person.
4. Never ask your three-year-old brother to hold a tomato.
5. You can't trust dogs to watch your food.
6. Don't sneeze when someone is cutting your hair.
7. Never hold a dust buster and a cat at the same time.
8. You can't hide a piece of broccoli in a glass of milk.
9. Don't wear polka-dot underwear with white shorts.
10. The best place to be when you're sad is Grandma's lap.

Part II: The Healing

The 12 Steps of Alcoholics Anonymous

1. We admitted we were powerless over alcohol—that our lives had become unmanageable.

2. Came to believe that a Power greater than ourselves could restore us to sanity.

3. Made a decision to turn our will and our lives over to the care of God as we understood Him.

4. Made a searching and fearless moral inventory of ourselves.

5. Admitted to God, to ourselves, and to another human being the exact nature of our wrongs.

6. Were entirely ready to have God remove all these defects of character.

7. Humbly asked Him to remove our shortcomings.

8. Made a list of all persons we had harmed, and became willing to make amends to them all.

9. Made direct amends to such people wherever possible, except when to do so would injure them or others.

10. Continued to take personal inventory and when we were wrong promptly admitted it.

11. Sought through prayer and meditation to improve our conscious contact with God as we understood Him, praying only for knowledge of His will for us and the power to carry that out.

12. Having had a spiritual awakening as a result of these steps, we tried to carry this message to others, and to practice these principles in all our affairs.

The First Step

Faith is taking the first step, even when you
don't see the whole staircase.
Martin Luther King[18]

~

STEP 1

Step 1: We admitted we were powerless over alcohol—that our lives had become unmanageable.

If we were going upstairs, we would start by putting a foot on the first step. Same with the 12 Steps of AA, Al-Anon, and the other programs that sprang from Alcoholics Anonymous.

We must have gotten over some of our denial; we have, to some extent, recognized that there is a problem—possibly we have even recognized that we were or are part of the problem. We may acknowledge that our denial has not been useful to us and that we'd like to get rid of it. How? We don't just learn to avoid denial; we need to understand it well enough to deal with it in our lives. We could say that we must "feel" it for the maximum benefit. Denial is one of those things that is so wrapped up with our emotions that this cannot be just an intellectual exercise. It is very difficult for me to say (and believe in my heart) that a situation is out of hand and that I cannot control it. This may sound like a statement of despair, but it is NOT. It is, rather, an acknowledgement of our human limitations.

Step 1 in all 12-Step programs is "We admitted we were powerless over [alcohol or drugs or gambling, etc.], that our lives had become unmanageable." Now this is a big chunk to grab on to. This is where we must deal with denial and let our minds overcome the

---

[18] Martin Luther King, Jr. (1929–1968), African-American leader, Nobel Prize winner (1964).

emotions that tell us we can do it all. We have to let go of the natural tendency to keep everything hidden, even from ourselves, and to recognize reality. To be ready to let someone else in to help where we are vulnerable. To acknowledge to ourselves that something is wrong in our lives, and that we don't have the power to do it all ourselves. And this can lead to true freedom.

WOW!!! Is this heavy stuff? Let's look at all the factors we have working here. First, we admitted we were powerless over the addiction. This means that we must have gotten at least partly over the denial that there is a problem. Now we also face the fact that we had no control over the behavior of the addicted person(s). We accept the concept that we are unable to "fix it."

If we get this far, we can look with awe at how far we have come. The reality is, however, that this epiphany usually doesn't come so quickly or easily. And what is clear at one moment often becomes cloudy again as the old thoughts and feelings try to maintain their dominance in our lives.

And now must we also say our lives are unmanageable? What great leaps of faith this entails. What soul searching and tearing apart of the old emotions and beliefs must be accomplished to reach this point. And once here, perhaps feeling naked and exposed, what have we accomplished? We have torn apart much of what we believed was right for what has often been a long period of time, and where do we go from here? Thankfully, this is only the beginning of a long process.

In this modern age of change, we frequently see some of the old and familiar torn down to make way for something new. Many an old landmark has disappeared under the wrecking ball, only to see a newer, higher, and hopefully more useful edifice constructed. Sometimes we wish for the old and familiar back, but if the new structure has been well thought out and the plans properly followed, the new will serve us better.

Change, even good change (like a marriage or the birth of a child), creates stress. So it is throughout our lives. And when they are followed to the best of our ability, the 12-Step programs have proven to be excellent plans for dealing with changes. But as with any worthwhile rebuilding project, there are prices to pay. One must deal with denial, have an awareness of what is really happening, and accept limitations.

Of course we will continue with the steps. The most common way of handling the steps is to take them in order. Just as a trip of a thousand miles begins with the first step, so there is logic in the order of these. However, the first three steps are often discussed together in meetings because they lay the foundation of our new building. These first three steps are clearing the land and pouring the foundation for our new structure. We need to keep in mind that we cannot put in the foundation until the land is cleared, nor can we put on the roof before the walls are there to support it. The 12 Steps are building blocks for a better life and must be taken in order, just as a building is erected from the bottom up.

◅☺▻

FROM DOG TO GOD

Dear God:

Here is a list of some of the things I must remember to be a good dog:

1. I will not eat the cat's food before he eats it.
2. I will not eat the cat's food after he throws it up.
3. I will not roll on dead seagulls, fish, crabs, etc., just because I like the way they smell.
4. The litter box is not a cookie jar.
5. The sofa is not a face towel.
6. The garbage collector is not stealing our stuff.
7. I don't need to suddenly stand straight up when I'm under the coffee table.
8. I must shake the rainwater out of my fur before entering the house—not after.
9. I will not come in from outside and immediately drag my butt across the carpet.
10. The cat is not a squeaky toy, so when I play with him and he makes that noise, it's usually not a good thing.

The Second Step

Such knowledge is too wonderful for me.
Psalm 139:6

~

STEP 2

Step 2: Came to believe that a Power greater than ourselves could restore us to sanity.

Now we've looked at denial and the necessity of breaking that habit. We have acknowledged that there is a problem. So what can we do about it?

Step 1 tells us that we are powerless over alcohol—and the disease of alcoholism/addiction. What? Who, me?! I am powerless over the disease of alcoholism? I don't have the power to control alcoholism and its effects? (Well, do you have the power to control cancer? Heart disease? A broken leg?) This is not much different. Of course, one could substitute the word *heroin* for *alcohol*. Or try cocaine, crack, pot, amphetamines, inhalants, and many more. You get the idea.

What does it mean that we are powerless? It simply means we DO NOT and CANNOT control this substance. This is exactly what most of us do NOT want to hear. I certainly should be able to control this thing that is ruining my son's/wife's/parent's/husband's/friend's/sibling's life. And the second part of the statement, that my life has become unmanageable, rubs salt into the wound. How is my life unmanageable when I am so competent, when I take care of everything? Were it not for me, the whole world would know what chaos we live in, the bills wouldn't get paid, the kids fed and clothed, etc., etc., etc.

However, a clear and searching look at my behavior may show me that I have, probably more than once, been out of control. Perhaps I prided myself that I held in my anger at the addict but then became enraged by some small thing. Perhaps I tried to take the focus off the alcoholic by behaving in ways I find unacceptable. Yes, my life is at times unmanageable.

So, I am powerless. My life is unmanageable. That is the bad news. Now for the good news. Step 2 tells me there is a Power greater than myself that can restore me to sanity. I am not dependent on my own resources alone. I can have access to the wisdom and guidance of a Power far greater than my puny human self.

Here is a hang-up for many of us. Do we have trouble with belief in a Power greater than ourselves? Do we balk at hearing that God stuff? Are we too afraid or too angry to trust anybody but ourselves? (But doing it by ourselves hasn't been all that satisfactory.) Have we prayed too many prayers that didn't seem to get answered?

Even those of us who practiced a formal religion were often disappointed in the result—we felt no comfort or solace. Our depression was too great to be healed by a few words spoken in a religious service.

In 12-Step programs, no one tells you to believe in God. Belief in ourselves alone hasn't done it, though, has it? Could there be something out there or in here that could guide and help us in the growing despair of our situation? Remembering that all 12-Step programs began with Alcoholics Anonymous (AA) and use the same steps, we can substitute words such as gambling, overeating, sex, pornography, and other behaviors to replace alcohol or other substances.

May we, for a moment, step out of our co-dependent situation to hear about the experience of some AA members:

> While attending a series of AA meetings, I watched one man (Ken) who was trying very hard to remain sober. Ken kept falling off the wagon, seemingly for no good reason. No family members were trying to sabotage him, he had taken part in a good rehab program, and he had a great deal of support from our group. I started listening closely to what he was saying in meetings and soon noted that he was in the "I" mode. His ego was in the way, and he believed he could do it all alone. He couldn't, or wouldn't, even accept the group conscience as a Higher Power. I saw him at a meeting where he again stated his lack of belief in any Power greater than himself.

However, his other friends were sure he had put it all together this time. Most of them were so sure he would make it this time that they were working very hard to convince me, the one that had predicted his fall in the past. After the meeting I asked his friend and employer how much money Ken had borrowed. The friend wondered why I was asking. I explained that without a Higher Power, I believed Ken would be going back out as soon as he could. He had borrowed a $100 advance from his then employer—who was also in the program and was at that meeting. His friend and employer was very sure Ken "had it" this time. But without a belief in something greater than himself, and with money in his pocket, Ken was out on the bar circuit the next day, and I never heard from him again.

George, AA member

Many members of 12-Step programs say they CAME, then they CAME TO, and finally they CAME TO BELIEVE. Thousands have found that Something. For some, the Higher Power was the group itself; after all, the combined wisdom and strength of the group is greater than that of any one member. A long, strong chain can be fabricated from many small links. Each link by itself can only reach a little way, but when combined with many others, the chain can grow and attain great distances. For some others, the Power might be an ideal, for still others, a phase of the natural world: the starry sky, a sturdy oak tree, the creative energy of the universe—anything outside ourselves. Eventually, most—not all—get to the place where they refer to "my Higher Power, whom I choose to call God." It's amazing how our lives—if not the things around us—can change for the better once we have come to believe in a "Power greater than ourselves."

"...that can restore us to sanity." Hey, wait a minute. What's this about sanity? Restore WHOM to sanity?? Not me. I'm the sane one. Oh? Really? Did you ever pour booze down the sink and fill the bottles with water? Did you ever make excuses for your kid to the school? Did you ever call the boss to report your spouse ill when it was a hangover? Did you ever do any bizarre thing to try to stop your loved one from drinking/drugging? Did any of this work? Could you possibly be an example of someone who fits the definition of insanity (doing the same thing over and over, expecting different results)? If so, welcome to the club. We were all insane to some degree. And nearly all of us who have found a program are getting better. You can, too.

<⊙⊳

WHY ATHLETES CAN'T HAVE REGULAR JOBS

1. New Orleans Saint RB George Rogers when asked about the up-coming season: "I want to rush for 1,000 or 1,500 yards, which-ever comes first."
2. Upon hearing Joe Jacobi of the 'Skins say: "I'd run over my own mother to win the Super Bowl," Matt Millen of the Raiders said: "To win, I'd run over Joe's Mom, too."
3. Torrin Polk, University of Houston receiver, on his coach, John Jenkins: "He treats us like men. He lets us wear earrings."
4. Football commentator and former player Joe Theismann: "No-body in football should be called a genius. A genius is a guy like Norman Einstein."
5. Senior basketball player at the University of Pittsburgh: "I'm go-ing to graduate on time, no matter how long it takes."
6. Bill Peterson, a Florida State football coach: "You guys line up alphabetically by height." And, "You guys pair up in groups of three, and then line up in a circle."
7. Boxing promoter Dan Duva on Mike Tyson going to prison: "Why would anyone expect him to come out smarter? He went to prison for three years, not Princeton."
8. Stu Grimson, Chicago Blackhawks left wing, explaining why he keeps a color photo of himself above his locker: "That's so when I forget how to spell my name, I can still find my clothes."
9. Lou Duva, veteran boxing trainer, on the Spartan training regi-men of heavyweight Andrew Golota: "He's a guy who gets up at six o'clock in the morning, regardless of what time it is."
10. Chuck Nevitt, North Carolina State basketball player, explaining to Coach Jim Valvano why he appeared nervous at practice: "My sister's expecting a baby, and I don't know if I'm going to be an uncle or an aunt.
11. Frank Layden, Utah Jazz president, on a former player: "I asked him, 'Son, what is it with you? Is it ignorance or apathy?' He said, 'Coach, I don't know and I don't care.'"
12. Shelby Metcalf, basketball coach at Texas A&M, recounting what he told a player who received four F's and one D: "Son, looks to me like you're spending too much time on one subject."
13. In the words of NC State great Charles Shackelford: "I can go to my left or right, I am amphibious."

The Third Step

There are more things in heaven and earth, Horatio, than are dreamt of in your philosophy.
Shakespeare, Hamlet

∽

STEP 3

Step 3: Made a decision to turn our will and our lives over to the care of God *as we understood Him*.

There are two elements here: first, turning our will over, and second, God. Both concepts can be overwhelming. Some find it hard to acknowledge God. One 12-Step program member says that to her, GOD is a code word for the Great Creative Life Force of the Universe. Some refer simply to a Higher Power.

We have acknowledged our own powerlessness with Step 1. After acknowledging powerlessness, there is some logic in looking to a Power greater than ourselves. A good look at the universe, or even at our insignificant planet, causes one to realize that there is some order in the scheme of things, some force at work keeping the planets in their orbits, the electrons in their orbits in the atoms of matter...you get the idea.

One of America's wisest men was Ralph Waldo Emerson. He had this to say: "A little consideration of what takes place around us every day would show us that a higher law than that of our will regulates events." Maybe so, but turning our lives, and especially our own will, over to anything outside ourselves—oh my, how hard that is! How hard it is to give up control, or in our case, the illusion of control. Yet we know we've been able to control little or nothing having to do with alcoholism. We might as well try to control cancer or heart disease or the weather.

This turning over will and life is an ongoing process. Many of us begin with the big problems, those we KNOW we have no choice about: the weather, the economy, major diseases. In such things, there is nowhere to turn but to a Power greater than ourselves. As we progress, we come to trust this Power, asking for guidance in large or small matters and becoming willing and open to receiving guidance and direction.

For some of us, DECISION is a major obstacle. We seem incapable of making any decisions. But if we take the steps in order, we first accept our inability to control the disease of alcoholism and addiction and our unmanageable life. Next we come to believe that a Power greater than ourselves can help. After taking these two steps, doesn't it seem desirable to take the next one, the giant leap to making the decision to turn it all over to the care of this Power? In our programs, some people describe this as:

- I can't.
- God can.
- I guess I'll let Him.

In turning my will and life over to the care of a Higher Power, I become receptive to guidance. This Power gives love and support that fills and surrounds me in my daily life. I do not have to earn it. I need do nothing to receive this care—I only need to be open and receptive to it. Some might call this GRACE. Once we receive such acceptance and love, we usually want to let it flow through us and out to others.

What are the obstacles to trusting in a Higher Power? Mainly the giving up of whatever control we imagine we have. Often it is that we want guarantees. Turning a situation over means I give up control of it. How do I know I will get my way?

If I want the benefits of a 12-Step spiritual program, I will have to take the risk and let go. Things may or may not turn out the way I want them to, but building a relationship with my Higher Power will help me grow into a strong, confident, loving person, a person capable of coping with whatever comes long after a particular crisis has been resolved. A wise member says she doesn't pray for things to turn out the way she wants, but that "whatever happens, [she] can handle it."

It has been said that forming a relationship with God gives us exactly what we want, "not at the time, or in the measure, or in the very thing desired, but joy and fulfillment far beyond anything we could ever dare ask."

Many, maybe most, of us do Step 3 over and over. Some of us gladly give it all to God at 5:30 a. m., but by 6:30 have taken it all back. Are we doomed to failure? No, we need to PRACTICE. We have made a start by making the DECISION to turn over our lives and will. We now have to keep at it, something like a dog worrying a bone. Perfecting Step 3 might be like perfecting any skill—we keep at it and keep getting better. After all, most of us fell off our bike many times before perfecting our balance so we could ride effortlessly. Practice makes perfect?? In this program, we strive for progress, NOT perfection.

Yes, making the decision to turn over our will and our lives means relinquishing control. It also means choosing between a sane life and an insane one. When we let go of insisting on our own will, we make a commitment to sanity. This can be followed by serenity.

We are making a new start. Who doesn't remember the Dr. Seuss story of the Grinch who stole Christmas? Dr. Seuss[19] himself told a couple of kids that the Grinch was the hero, saying, "It's not where you start that's important, but where you finish." Starting now, we can make a brand new finish for ourselves!

Most of us do find it REALLY hard to turn over our will and life to the care of a Higher Power. We're scared of losing control, of being out of control—ha, where do we think we were? Why not give this new way a try? Someone compared surrender to the Higher Power to ballroom dancing—one person leads, one follows. When both try to lead, there are awkward movements, but when one partner can relax and follow, the other can do the steering and the pair glides easily over the dance floor.

Turning over my problems does not release me from my responsibilities. I have tools to use in building and maintaining my life, like intelligence, judgment, reason, and the Power to detach. "Turning it over" involves quiet listening and acting on guidance received. You've heard the old saying that "God helps those who help themselves." Members of Al-Anon sometimes put it this way: "You give it to GOD, but YOU do the legwork."

On the subject of what can happen by turning your problems over and seeking guidance from the Higher Power, we turn to Ralph Waldo Emerson. He said, "There is guidance for each of us and by lowly listening we shall hear the right word. Certainly there is a

---

[19] Theodor Seuss Geisel (1904–1991), children's author and cartoonist.

right for you that needs no choice on your part. Place yourself in the middle of the stream of power and wisdom which flows into your life. Then without effort you are impelled to truth and perfect contentment."

Remember, only you can make it a great day.

CONCLUSIONS

For those of you who watch what you eat, here's the final word on nutrition and health. It's a relief to know the truth after all those conflicting nutritional studies.

1. The Japanese eat very little fat and suffer fewer heart attacks than Americans.
2. The Mexicans eat a lot of fat and suffer fewer heart attacks than Americans.
3. The Chinese drink very little red wine and suffer fewer heart attacks than Americans.
4. The Italians drink a lot of red wine and suffer fewer heart attacks than Americans.
5. The Germans drink a lot of beer and eat lots of sausages and fats and suffer fewer heart attacks than Americans.

CONCLUSION:
Eat and drink what you like. Speaking English is apparently what kills you.

The Fourth and Fifth Steps

Know thyself.
Inscribed in the forecourt of the Temple of Apollo at Delphi

Man: "What is difficult?"
Thales: "To know thyself"
Thales[20]

No man is the worse for knowing the worst of himself.
Thomas Fuller[21]

∽

STEP 4

Step 4: Made a searching and fearless moral inventory of ourselves.

What is an inventory? Think of a grocery store. You inventory your stock occasionally to see if your produce section might have more than enough celery but not enough kumquats. Or if the bakery is overstocked with double chocolate fudge peanut butter bagels and understocked with sunflower seed whole wheat bread. Or if the pharmacy is long on Ex-Lax but short on Prozac.

So a personal inventory shows us where we stand. It's not just a tool to root out our weaknesses and shortcomings, but it shows us our strengths and decencies as well.

It helps most people to make a written inventory. Why? It is something we do over a period of time, and it's often helpful to look back on what we felt beginning our inventory and how we feel now.

---

[20]Thales (~625 BC–547 BC).
[21]Thomas Fuller (1654–1734).

Most of us are inclined to forget such things, and a written list jogs the memory.

An inventory begins with a commitment to rigorous honesty. Identifying a problem is the first step toward solving it. What tools do we use for our inventory? In the grocery store we'll use a pad and pencil—or some electronic gadget that does the same thing. In a Step 4 inventory, we need these and, more important, some idea of what we are looking for. Most people who have come this far seek guidance from their Higher Power in being truthful and loving as they sift through memories and feelings. Some people begin an inventory by listing memories of people, events, institutions, beliefs, and circumstances that trigger positive or negative feelings: sadness, joy, fear, remorse, neglect, care, anger, resentment. Some items appear on the list more than once and this is normal. At this point, the job is not to analyze or judge, just to be thorough.

Some people put the events in their lives in a sort of chronological order: grades in school, where they lived, significant relationships of the time. Others just start brainstorming. Naturally they don't remember everything at once—this is why writing is valuable.

Then, with their Higher Power's help, some organize a table or chart with columns under headings, or a page for each entry on their list, writing answers in each of the categories, such as:

- Incident: what happened?
- Effect: on self/others,
- Feelings: at the time/now, and
- Self-examination: attitudes of self-pity, self-will, self-deception, pride.

And don't forget the times you acted right! Some people are afraid someone else will look at their inventory, so they are uncomfortable about putting it on paper. This is a legitimate concern and is something to be addressed with the Higher Power's help.

There is no need to rush through an inventory, but since the journey of a thousand miles begins with that one step, it's good to get started. Since no one is perfect, probably no one has ever done a perfect Step 4 inventory. But as one recovering alcoholic says:

> I was in such great fear of doing the Fourth Step because I was afraid of finding out I was truly a bad person. After all, I had been lying and making false excuses for my horrible behavior to the point that now that I was getting sober, I realized the extent and consequences of my behavior and I felt terrible for the way I had been treating my family and

others. But much to my surprise, I found that I was not as bad as I had first thought, and I felt a great relief when I finished the Fourth Step and got it out in the open, like making a confession and letting go of all the old stuff and realizing I could now do better and knew what I needed to avoid.

Len said that he identified with what Aldous Huxley[22] said in *The Perennial Philosophy*: "If most of us remain ignorant of ourselves, it is because self-knowledge is painful and we prefer the pleasures of illusion." But once we face our own self-knowledge, we can do much better and gain some humility and insight.

STEP 5

Step 5: Admitted to God, to ourselves, and to another human being the exact nature of our wrongs.

> Unless we can bear self-mortification, we shall not be able to carry self-examination to the necessary painful lengths. Without humility, there can be no illuminating self-knowledge.
> Arnold Toynbee,[23] A Study of History, 1961

As we can see, Step 5 logically follows Step 4. We have admitted our wrongs to God and to ourselves—sometimes we find we've done more hurt to ourselves than we thought. Now we need to find another human being to make the step complete. And just not any human being. Aunt Millicent, the town gossip, would not be a good choice. Nor would rigidly judgmental Uncle Fritz. A counselor might be a good choice—a counselor familiar with the family disease of alcoholism. Or some trusted friend from Al-Anon. Clergy are sometimes a good choice, but here caution is in order. A priest or minister who knows nothing of the disease nature of alcoholism might feel the need to be tough and judgmental, which is usually not in our best interest.

We are advised to take Step 5 as soon as possible. To not do so would be like acknowledging an infected wound without cleansing it. Part of Step 4 involved recognizing patterns of negative thoughts and emotions. Our thoughts—the only things we have power to control—have sent us down some awful roads. Remember, the thought comes first, then the words or actions. We know we need to control our thoughts so they won't control us. Out of control thoughts are like a car, uncontrolled by its driver, weaving crazily and smacking

---

[22] Aldous Huxley (1894–1963).
[23] Arnold Toynbee (1899–1975), historian.

cones or barrels or pedestrians. Controlling our thoughts is no easy thing, but it gets easier, and with continual practice, we enter a new life of talking and living the truth.

FISHIN'

Earl and Bubba are quietly sitting in a boat fishing, chewing tobacco and drinking beer when suddenly Bubba says,

"Think I'm gonna divorce the wife—she ain't spoke to me in over two months." Earl spits overboard, takes a long, slow sip of beer and says,

"Better think it over...women like that are hard to find."

The Sixth and Seventh Steps

A new heart will I give you and a new spirit will I put within you.
Ezekiel 36:26

All I know is there is a God and I ain't Him.
Heard in AA

~

STEP 6

Step 6: Were entirely ready to have God remove all these defects of character.

Addicted people who begin recovery often find that, although they may not be participating in the addiction any longer, they are not really OK. They have come a long way, but there are still things that make them less than what they want to be—call them character defects—and just putting down a bottle or a pipe or clicking off the porn site doesn't erase those defects. Does the Bible verse from Ezekiel above sound like the Higher Power is telling us it's OK, that character defects can be erased? Many have found that this is so. They became ready—we might even call it willing—to be changed, and these defects were removed.

Can this apply to us, the co-dependents? We probably know by now that we were about as insane as the addicted ones and with as many shortcomings, albeit without addiction. One alcoholic used to say to her husband, "I act this way because I am an alcoholic. What's your excuse?"

Do we also need to be ready to have our defects removed? Do we cling to our defects like revenge, self-pity, and pride? Most of us find we enjoy them—maybe as much as the alcoholic enjoys the booze. But are they doing us any good? Are they a waste of time? Would we be better off rid of them?

Step 6 is one of change, of becoming ready to grow. Discomfort with our thoughts and behavior is part of this readiness. Readiness could—but usually doesn't—come in a sudden flash of enlightenment, but more often it comes with a little progress in a positive direction. Remember, Al-Anon is a program of "progress, not perfection."

We get to cooperate with God, to become ready to let go of our faults and imperfections, and then let God take care of the rest.

STEP 7

Step 7: Humbly asked Him to remove our shortcomings.

All the steps—and, indeed the whole program—require some humility. Yet this is the only step that directly mentions it. It's the first word. It smacks us between the eyes. It tells us we cannot remove our own pride, misdeeds, and shortcomings. We must surrender to God and allow Him to do it for us.

In Step 7, we abandon the idea that we can do it by ourselves. We finally accept life on life's terms—or on God's terms. When we put everything into God's hands, we have done all we can. Sort of reminds us of the chapter in *Winnie the Pooh* where Piglet is entirely surrounded by water and puts a note in a bottle saying, "Help. Piglet. Me," and throws the bottle out into the flood, knowing he has done everything he can to save himself.

In Step 7, we accept the fact that we need help in being restored to sanity. We're asking God to take away what we don't need; taking away our defects makes room for our assets to shine forth. Our shortcomings are blocks that prevent us from reaching our true potential and distance us from our Higher Power.

> Humility...means seeing myself in true
> relationship to my fellow man and God.
> Lois W., founder of Al-Anon

> Humility may be quietness of heart; we do
> our part and trust God to do the rest.

<⊙>

WATCH FOR THESE CONSOLIDATIONS LATER THIS YEAR

1. Hale Business Systems, Mary Kay Cosmetics, Fuller Brush, and W. R. Grace Co. will merge and become: Hale, Mary, Fuller, Grace
2. Polygram Records, Warner Bros., and Zesta Crackers join forces and become: Poly, Warner Cracker
3. 3M will merge with Goodyear and become: MMMGood.
4. Zippo Manufacturing, Audi Motors, Dofasco, and Dakota Mining will merge and become: ZipAudiDoDa
5. FedEx is expected to join its competitor, UPS, and become: FedUP
6. Fairchild Electronics and Honeywell Computers will become: Fairwell Honeychild.
7. Knotts Berry Farm and the National Organization of Women will become: Knott NOW!

The Eighth, Ninth, and Tenth Steps

Hard though it may be to accept, remember that guilt is sometimes a friendly internal voice reminding you that you are messing up.
Marge Kennedy[24]

Guilt, the gift that keeps on giving.
Erma Bombeck[25]

∼

STEP 8

Step 8: Made a list of all persons we had harmed, and became willing to make amends to them all.

Addicted people have destructive lifestyles that are like a tornado that sweeps through their lives, leaving great wreckage. We feel that we are part of that wreckage. We are the innocent victims of the whirlwind. Or are we? Is it possible that we have left a bit of wreckage of our own? Think about it. Many of us have found that we have done great damage to our children, other family members, the addicted one(s), AND ourselves. Some folks feel that their own names belong at the top of the list.

Here, again, it is best to put the list in writing. Oddly, we may find our thoughts and feelings changing as we take this step. We may see extenuating circumstances or we may realize that there is a different way to look at a situation. Or we may see that we were truly behaving like a jerk. But our job in Step 8 is to make a list of people we have harmed by what we have done or left undone. It is about us.

---

[24] Marge Kennedy, U.S. writer.
[25] Erma Bombeck (1927–1996), U.S. humorist.

This Step is a way to release ourselves from guilt. When we see the memories and pain written out right in front of us, we may see them as almost manageable. Maybe they are not totally overwhelming. Perhaps we can let our hurts and resentments go. In Step 8, all we have to do is make a list. Oh yes, and "become WILLING to make amends..."

Uh-oh, there's the 'W' word again. We must become WILLING to make amends. That can be a sticky wicket. Sometimes it's hard to give up our pain and suffering, even though we're told doing so will make us feel better. Our resentments are sooo justified, they are so a part of us, who we are.

Some have found it helpful to make more than one list. There would be the list of persons "I would never, not at any time, under any circumstances, be willing to make amends to," and a list of persons "I might, possibly, sometime, somewhere be willing to make amends to," and a list of persons "I might consider making amends to," and a list of persons "I could, even now, make amends to."

Hey, do we want to give others power over us, power that doesn't belong to them? That is exactly what we do when we hold on to grudges, resentments, and ill will. Picture giving a person a big, heavy chain and allowing the person to wrap it around us and jerk on it to pull us where they want us to go. We are NOT FREE if we allow that. Remember that in giving up resentment against a person, we cease giving that person power over us; we are closer to giving up our victim status. Remember, too, that we are usually forgiven in about the same measure that we are willing to forgive. Above all, remember that our Higher Power wants us to succeed and is there to help us with our list—and with the difficult Step 9 coming next.

STEP 9

Step 9: Made direct amends to such people wherever possible, except when to do so would injure them or others.

It is the highest form of self-respect to admit our errors and make amends for them.
Dale Turner[26]

Don't let your pride or lack of courage stand in the way of saying you're sorry to people you may have offended.
Sean Covey[27]

---

[26] Dale Turner, character in the TV show "Jericho."
[27] Sean Covey (b. 1964), U.S. author, speaker, consultant, management expert, author of *The Seven Habits of Highly Effective People*.

To take Step 9, we need courage, sensitivity, and good judgment. We also need a sense of timing; we should not be impulsive or careless, which could make matters worse. Here's another place where we can use help from our Higher Power. Humility and honesty can repair damaged relationships when we make reasonable efforts to meet those we have offended. We let them know we are approaching them to make amends. If they prefer not to meet with us, we respect their wishes. We approach each person in a spirit of humility and reconciliation, never self-justification.

There are situations where it is not possible to make direct amends. If a person has died or moved and left no forwarding address, we can make indirect amends. We may write a letter of apology, even though it will never be delivered. We might give (anonymously) to their favorite charity or anonymously do something for a family member. Above all, we change our behavior so this will not be an issue in the future.

This step states that we make direct amends...except when to do so would injure them or others. How do we know if this will be the case? There are those who have ducked making amends to some people with the excuse that doing so would be injurious. Here again, we need the assistance of our Higher Power. If we have deprived someone of a material thing, we need to acknowledge our wrongdoing and make full restitution. We must make the first move in healing a rift between ourselves and our relatives/friends/neighbors/employers. Even if their share of blame is greater, this overture benefits us. It is our sanity we are restoring, and our serenity we are bringing to our own lives.

> We all find peace if we forgive.
> Danielle Rosenblatt[28]

> The best way to make amends is to not do it again.
> Anonymous

STEP 10

Step 10: Continued to take personal inventory and when we were wrong promptly admitted it.

> In politics...never retreat, never react, never admit a mistake.
> Emperor Napoleon Bonaparte[29]

---

[28] Danielle Rosenblatt, children's author of *The Ant in the Cellar*.
[29] Napoleon Bonaparte (1769–1821), French general, politician, emperor.

This may work well for the emperor, although Napoleon did not stay emperor as long as he'd planned. For us, this advice might be better:

> When you make a mistake admit it, correct it,
> and learn from it immediately.
> Stephen R. Covey[30]

> The man with insight enough to admit his
> limitations comes nearest to perfection.
> Johann Wolfgang von Goethe[31]

If nothing else, people who can quickly admit mistakes are more popular than those who can't. One woman relates that, at a time when her teenage daughter couldn't stand her, she heard the girl on the phone with a friend saying: "The one good thing about my mother is she will admit it when she's wrong."

The idea of Step 10—and many of the others—seems quite unnatural, at least in our present society. Why would we want to admit errors, anyhow? When asked, "Would you rather be right or be happy?" the answer is usually, "Don't be silly. Of course I'd rather be right." But after more consideration, happy looks pretty good, even better.

One Al-Anon member didn't think much of Step 10, if she thought of it at all. But as she progressed, she came to realize:

> This Step is SO freeing. I never imagined the freedom I would have when I could immediately say I was wrong, I was sorry, whatever was appropriate to the situation. I no longer needed to get my hackles up or try to disappear and hope my goof would soon be forgotten. Now when I'm wrong, I say so, with no attempt to justify my actions or make excuses. And most of the time, this is acceptable. I've saved time and maybe a friendship or two.

> Shannon, Al-Anon member

Considering these steps of what might be termed reconciliation, Step 10 could be the icing on the cake, the roof on the house. It ties up the other two. We don't now have to agonize over our guilt and wonder how to go about making our amends. We have made our list

---

[30] Stephen R. Covey (b. 1932), U.S. motivational author of *The Seven Habits of Highly Effective Teens* and *The Seven Habits of Happy Kids*.

[31] Johann Wolfgang von Goethe (1749–1832), German playwright, poet, novelist, dramatist.

and, as far as possible, made our amends. Now we continue taking personal inventory: morning, evening, as often as we need to. This keeps us from slipping back into our old, unproductive ways.

One day at a time we check ourselves, our actions and reactions, our attitudes and thoughts. We see where we may need to make a correction. Like airline pilots, we are always making little corrections in our course, knowing that just getting a bit off course now can put us way off in getting to our destination.

◁ ☺ ▷

SISTER MARY ANN'S GASOLINE

Sister Mary Ann, who worked for a home health agency, was out making her rounds visiting homebound patients when she ran out of gas. As luck would have it, a Texaco gasoline station was just a block away.

She walked to the station to borrow a gas can and buy some gas. The attendant told her that the only gas can he owned had been loaned out, but she could wait until it was returned. Since Sister Mary Ann was on the way to see a patient, she decided not to wait and walked back to her car.

She looked for something in her car that she could fill with gas and spotted the bedpan she was taking to the patient. Always resourceful, Sister Mary Ann carried the bedpan to the station, filled it with gasoline, and carried the full bedpan back to her car.

As she was pouring the gas into her tank, two Baptists watched from across the street. One of them turned to the other and said, "If it starts, I'm turning Catholic!!"

The Eleventh Step

There are many ways to pray, as there are many ways to God.
James Dillet Freeman

STEP 11

Step 11: Sought through prayer and meditation to improve our conscious contact with God *as we understood Him*, praying only for knowledge of His will for us and the power to carry that out.

This chapter will deal with prayer, including what it is, some ways people pray, and how one who doesn't believe in God might pray.

The dictionary is a good place to go for definitions, so here's what the New Webster's Expanded Dictionary has to say: prayer (n.) One who prays; the act of praying; a petition; a solemn petition to God; a formula of worship, public or private; that part of a written petition which specifies the thing desired to be granted.

Somehow, this definition seems like more than we need here. Why don't we just say that prayer is the communication between an individual and that individual's Higher Power? Some people are turned off to prayer because they think it's just asking some cantankerous old guy in the sky for a lot of stuff He doesn't want to give us and that it doesn't work.

CONCENTRATION

Larry Dossey, MD,[32] has studied prayer's effects on healing illnesses for quite a few years. His reports of scientific studies on this are astounding. But that's another story. Dossey tells of a surgeon who said he had long ago given up prayer. Dossey pointed out that

---

[32] Larry Dossey (b. 1940), former Chief of Staff, Humana Medical City, Dallas; author of ten books on role of consciousness and spirituality in healing.

during surgery this man experienced total concentration. He was completely immersed in the operation; he, the scalpel, and the patient were blended into one entity. This could be a form of prayer.

Often people enter 12-Step programs without a belief in God. Usually before long they come to acknowledge the existence of a power greater than themselves (Step 2) and usually—but not always—get to the point of referring to "my Higher Power, whom I choose to call God." Along the way, some use the group conscience as their Higher Power, while others use an ideal such as truth or beauty or something in nature—a tree, the ocean, the sky.

How would a person who doesn't acknowledge God pray? One Al-Anon member said she had a big picture window in her bedroom with an unobstructed view of the sky. Viewing it at all times and seasons gave her a feeling of awe and wonder. She could look at the vastness and grandeur of the heavens and feel connected to the majesty and power of the universe. It gave her a sense of her place in the grand scheme of things, and when she was struggling with a problem, this contemplation gave her a sense of peace, and she could get answers.

For those whose Higher Power is the group conscience, the group is more powerful than individual members and careful listening can bring peace and the feeling of being connected to a wisdom and power greater than our own.

PRAY FOR WHAT?

"Be careful what you pray for. You might get it." Most of us have prayed for things that, when we got them, weren't really what we wanted. So we need to be careful that we are truly praying for things that will benefit us and help us along our road to recovery.

> We, ignorant of ourselves,
> Beg often our own harms, which the Wise Power
> Denies us for our own good; so we find profit
> By losing of our prayers.

> Shakespeare, *Antony and Cleopatra*

So what—if anything—should we pray for? Step 11 tells us to pray for knowledge of God's will for us and for the power to carry it out. These 12-Step programs emphasize the idea of praying only for guidance, realizing that we don't always know what we want and surely don't always know what's best for us. Prayer is NOT saying, "Hey, God, MY will, not THINE, be done." Yet, this is what many of us do, giving God instructions and a laundry list of our wishes or

80

demands. It's best not to give directions to God but to listen for and follow His directions to us.

FIRST THINGS FIRST

We wouldn't get out of bed and go straight to work, would we? We'd at least take off our pajamas, put on our clothes, and brush our teeth first. These things take a little time but are necessary to start our day. Maybe it's equally necessary to do what Step 11 says and take the time for prayer and meditation, to reach out and make contact with the power greater than ourselves. Rushing off for the day without this step may be akin to taking off for work in our bedclothes with mossy teeth.

The topic of prayer will come up again later on in this book because it is very important; we'll also touch on the Serenity Prayer and tell you about two rather unorthodox prayers that were entirely appropriate for the people and their circumstances.

◁☺▷

ABOUT CATS

Q: What is a cat's favorite dessert?
A: Mice pudding.

Q: How do you get milk from a cat?
A: Steal its saucer.

Q: What do you call someone who steals cats?
A: A purr-snatcher.

Q: What do you get if you cross a hungry cat and a canary?
A: A cat that isn't hungry any more

Q: Why did the silly kid try to feed pennies to the cat?
A: Because his mother told him to put money in the kitty.

Q: What do you call a cat that does tricks?
A: A magic kit.

Q: What kind of work does a weak cat do?
A: Light mouse work.

Q: Why did the Mama cat put stamps on her kittens?
A: She wanted to mail a litter.

The Twelfth Step

When you lift someone up a hill, you find yourself closer to the top.
Brownie Wise[33]

STEP 12

Step 12: Having had a spiritual awakening as a result of these steps, we tried to carry this message to others, and to practice these principles in all our affairs.

Step 12 is one of service. We have had a spiritual awakening. For a few, it comes as a blinding flash of light, but for most it's a little enlightenment here and a bit more there. In time we feel that we have been awakened and want to share our good fortune with others. We want everyone to have what we have.

I wanted to give the Program to all who needed it, which was most of the people I knew. I got my plunger and rammed it down their throats. After all, it was so good for them. In time I realized this might be doing more harm than good. As I pushed, they pushed back. Now, I still want everyone who needs it to have it, but I'm more subtle. I try to be an example of what Al-Anon can do. After all, Al-Anon is a program of "attraction, rather than promotion."
Jeanne, Al-Anon member

We do often feel ourselves filled with missionary zeal, just like those in other centuries who sailed away to spend a lifetime giving service and sharing their message. But as Jeanne said, ours

---

[33] Brownie Wise (1913–1992), saleswoman extraordinaire, vice-president of Tupperware, founder of Tupperware parties, first woman on the cover of *Business Week*.

is a program of attraction rather than promotion. Our behavior is our best selling point.

Here's how one teacher learned to share:

> Although I was unaware of it at the time, I had a spiritual awakening. Like many teachers, I could see some of the damage brought on by the addiction of a parent to alcohol/other drugs. We saw it as a bad thing, bad for the kids, something somebody ought to do something about and why don't they? To me it was a situation of them and us. I don't know just when or how it happened, but I did realize my family had the problem too, so it was not them and us, it was just us.
>
> Later, in Al-Anon, I tried to share the message. I was careful. I didn't come on like Gangbusters—that could've gotten me in a lot of trouble. When a parent shared a story of problems caused by the "Big A," I would tell my story and what was so helpful to me. No one responded. But often, a few years later, a parent would say, "You know, Miss D, I got into Al-Anon and my life is a lot better."
>
> Daffy, Al-Anon member

We often meet people whose lives have been affected by the "Big A," people at work, on the bus, in the neighborhood. There are opportunities to share what has been so useful to us. To share the realization that we are not alone, that there is a Power greater than ourselves, and that surrendering ourselves to this Power gives us a freedom from anxiety over our lives and our loved one—not that we don't have anxiety and even fear, but we know we are supported and sustained and that whatever happens, we can handle it.

> All will be well and all will be well and
> all that matters will be well.
> Hildegard of Bingen[34]

Part of our awakening is realizing that the Program works, but YOU have to work it.

---

[34]Hildegard of Bingen (1098–1179), German nun, writer, composer, philosopher, Christian mystic.

◁ ☺ ▷
EXERCISE FOR PEOPLE OVER 40

Begin by standing on a comfortable surface where you have plenty of room at each side.

With a five-pound potato bag in each hand, extend your arms straight out from your sides and hold them there as long as you can. Try to reach a full minute, and then relax.

Each day you'll find that you can hold this position for just a bit longer. After a couple of weeks, move up to ten-pound potato bags.

Then try fifty-pound potato bags and then eventually try to get to where you can lift a hundred-pound potato bag in each hand and hold your arms straight for more than a full minute. (I'm at this level.)

Then after you feel confident at this level, put a potato in each bag.

Part III:
How We Made It

The Secret Weight

Nothing weighs on us so heavily as a secret.
Jean De La Fontaine[35]

"Loose lips sink ships."

Have you ever heard that phrase before? It happens to be a slogan used during World War II to encourage people to keep their mouths shut regarding any information that could possibly be of use to the enemy. Those who remember or have studied World War II know it as a time of many secrets. The future of the world was in a delicate balance and a madman named Adolph Hitler was trying to control the next thousand years of civilization. His Third Reich was enveloping the world and, as with many movements, a scapegoat was desirable. The Jewish people were a group that had been used as a scapegoat before, and it was easy to point the finger of blame and hate at them. Jews were doing well as a people in Europe and many, both inside and outside of Germany, wanted to see the "different" people fall and the "great" ones take over some of their position and wealth. After all, they had killed Jesus and deserved whatever they got, didn't they?

So the trains started to Auschwitz and Dachau and Bergen-Belsen with their loads of human cargo destined for unspeakable evil, all for the crime of being Jewish. Some—possibly most—Germans knew something was going on. But the truth was so terrible that it was denied. Denial is a means of not dealing with unpleasant things. Most of us have done it, haven't we? So it became expedient for those who could do so to hide their Jewish ancestry. This

---

[35] Jean De La Fontaine (1621–1695), French poet, famous for his fables.

knowledge, in the wrong hands, would bring disaster upon their families. They must keep this dangerous secret from getting out or face a one-way trip to the gas chambers. What a terrible burden, to know that the government was looking over records to determine if any Jews were being missed.

And what if a friend or relative had Jewish blood? Should people turn them in, as the law demanded? Should they obey the law of the land? Were they responsible for the life of another? What was the cost of keeping this secret? What was their duty? And to whom?

So much for the secrets of Europe in the mid-twentieth century. Fast forward to the 1980s. The plague of the twentieth century was upon us. AIDS was just beginning to sweep through Africa with fallout on other continents as well. In the U.S., it was the time of the Ray brothers[36] and Ryan White.[37] The horrors of the disease and the mystery of how it was contracted conspired to make even compassionate folks shun its victims and their families. From the vantage point of the early twenty-first century, knowing what we now do about the transmission of AIDS—especially how it is NOT transmitted—it is hard to remember what it was like for families of those affected by this modern leprosy. To anyone wanting to understand how it was then, the book *Burden of a Secret* by Jimmy Allen[38] puts it out there with all the misery caused not only by the disease, but also by the strain and stress of keeping the secret.

A kindergarten teacher tells how it was when her hemophiliac sons were diagnosed with AIDS in 1987:

> When my sons crossed the line from HIV to full-blown AIDS, I knew there would be a challenge to keep anyone from finding out. There was the stigma of AIDS being a "not nice" disease, a disease whose victims were drug addicts or homosexuals. With our family, this was not the issue, but anyone was fair game for ostracism. AIDS was a disease too horrible to contemplate and one to be avoided at all costs.

---

[36] Ray brothers: Ricky (1977–1992), Robert (1978–2000), and Randy (b. 1973). These brothers fought to keep going to school despite their disease but had to move from their home in Arcadia, Florida, when somebody set fire to their house in 1987 after the court ruled that they could stay in school.

[37] Ryan White (1971–1990), a hemophiliac who contracted HIV from a contaminated blood treatment and harassed by other parents to keep him from attending school with their children.

[38] Reverend Dr. Jimmy R. Allen, Baptist minister, ethicist, humanitarian.

How it spread was clear; what was unclear was how it did NOT spread. I remember reading a statement by a doctor saying he didn't think AIDS could be contracted from a drinking glass, but he could not be certain. Any wonder that people would go to any length to avoid contact with anyone who could possibly be infectious?

If my children had a teacher who might be carrying a terrible disease, of course I would want that teacher kept away from them, whatever else might be in the teacher's favor. I didn't blame parents or administrators for getting rid of me, if it became known that my sons, through me, might spread AIDS to their children.

Being a long-time teacher with tenure, the Board of Education couldn't just get rid of me. But I'd be out of the classroom and probably put in some dismal office with little human contact.

During this time, I had a bike accident and the emergency room staff had me scheduled for surgery until a chest X-ray showed a lung spot. It was an abnormality that had been there at least twenty years, but right away they suspected tuberculosis and whisked me into a small room and closed the door. Anytime someone came to check me, I had to put on a mask that caused an allergic reaction. I was treated differently than I had been when I first arrived. No longer was the total concern to take care of my injuries, but even more, to keep from getting what I might be carrying.

This was a traumatic experience and also a taste of what could happen and might be happening to my sons.

My husband and I told NO ONE about our sons' diagnosis. We were so paranoid, we didn't even tell our daughter for a year and a half. (We, our sons, and our daughter lived in different states.)

Both boys died in 1992. Mike was buried on St. Patrick's Day and John on New Year's Eve. That summer, we became very hopeful, hearing that the HIV virus had been mapped and it was only a matter of time until a drug would be found to combat it—the Magic Bullet that might save our remaining son.

Still, we avoided any disclosure of our involvement with the disease. In September, after Arthur Ashe[39] had made

[39] Arthur Ashe (1943–1993), first African-American to compete at highest level of tennis, crusader for equality and awareness.

the public pronouncement of his AIDS and it was pretty much accepted that HIV/AIDS was not transmitted in any casual way, we told our family and friends, including my school.

Everyone was supportive, making it easier when John died. My colleagues couldn't have been more wonderful. From January, when I returned from John's funeral, until the end of school in June, someone gave us dinner every night and almost daily people gave us little gifts or cards. This support, along with a bereaved parents' group and Al-Anon made the difficult time a bit easier to endure.

Would I have done things differently? No. I still believe this was the only way. I did regret not being totally honest, although I don't recall any outright lying—just evasions.

More recently, I was diagnosed with breast cancer. What a relief to not have to keep it secret! In the joy of being able to talk about it freely, I told everybody, doubtless some who had no need or desire to hear it.

Daffy

This is an example of a situation in which most people would consider it desirable to keep the secret. Desirable or not, such secrecy does take a toll. Are there other situations in which the weight of secrecy is neither desirable nor healthy?

The next chapter will continue with secrets.

And that's no secret.

◁☺▷

ONE DOG TO ANOTHER

When my people go away, I bark and bark and bark and bark
'til they come back. Works every time!

DOG DIARY

7:00 a.m. Dog food! My favorite thing.
8:00 a.m. A car ride! My favorite thing.
8:40 a.m. A walk in the park! My favorite thing.
10:30 a.m. Got rubbed and petted! My favorite thing.
12:00 p.m. Lunch! My favorite thing.
1:30 p.m. Played in the yard! My favorite thing.
3:00 p.m. Chased a squirrel! My favorite thing.
5:00 p.m. Milk Bones! My favorite thing.
7:00 p.m. Got to play ball! My favorite thing.
8:00 p.m. Watched TV with my people! My favorite thing.
11:00 p.m. Sleeping on the bed! My favorite thing.

More About Secrets

*Camouflage is a game we all like to play, but our secrets
are as surely revealed by what we want to seem to be
as by what we want to conceal.*
Russell Lynes[40]

We are as sick as our secrets.
Al-Anon saying

In the last chapter, we spoke of secrets and the need to keep them under certain circumstances. We mentioned the situation of being a Jew in Nazi Germany or the family of an AIDS victim in the 1980s.

A more timeless secret, one probably around from the beginning, is that of family abuse. Only recently, thanks partly to Oprah and some others, physical, emotional, and even sexual abuse has been brought out into the open. Even so, how many of us are willing to shout from the housetops that this happens in OUR family?

We certainly don't want others to think our family is different, in a horrible sort of way, from theirs. Some of us go to great lengths to keep anyone from finding out what is happening behind the walls of our home. Alcohol or other drugs can make any problem worse. Even without abuse, the family where addiction rules is likely to lock their secrets tighter than the first atom bomb; if somehow the secret gets out, it will one day explode.

While secrecy may be essential in the situations previously given, there are times when it may not be in our best interest. Sometimes, although it's difficult, it is better to bring the secret out and, as the vacuum cleaner folks tell us: suck it up and deal with it.

---

[40] Russell Lynes (1910–1991), American art historian, photographer, editor, author.

> Oh, what a tangled web we weave
> When first we practice to deceive.
> Sir Walter Scott[41]

And there lies one of the problems. Sir Walter Scott was right. Keeping secrets often involves telling lies, maybe not big ones, maybe just a little evasion here and a half-truth there. Whenever we do something like this, there is the burden on us to be consistent. What we say on Monday can't be contradicted on Thursday and what we tell George can't be different from what we tell Frances. This can be pretty stressful after awhile, especially over a lifetime.

An example in an alcoholic home is calling in to work for the spouse (or parent or child) saying he or she is too ill to come to work when, in truth, the person is hanging over the toilet bowl getting rid of the last vestiges of last night's party. Another example is making the house look perfect to show that there is nothing wrong with this family; it is all-important to maintain the façade of cleanliness, respectability, and normalcy. The family mantra is: we must look good! The repercussions can also come out in a child who overachieves in order to take the focus off the family member who is acting in a socially unacceptable way. On the opposite extreme is the child whose outrageous behavior puts the spotlight on himself or herself to take it off the parent. There are other ways families handle this, some more bizarre than others.

You've heard the old story of the elephant in the living room. Everyone knows it is there but won't talk about it. They walk around the elephant, hang coats on the tusks, use the tail as a shoe brush and, when necessary, sweep up the elephant dung and dump it in the garden. The family has become so accustomed to the beast that they make adjustments and go about their business as though it isn't there.

So, should we go to the other extreme and blab everything to everybody? There was a little girl who was removed to a foster home because of sexual abuse. In her new school, she entertained the kindergarteners with stories of being raped by her uncle. The school social worker had the challenge of encouraging the child to share her experience, but only at the appropriate time and place.

As adults, we also need to use wisdom in our choice of the time and place to air our secrets. Again, counseling is a place to get things off our chest. A good counselor is accepting and non-judgmental and

---

[41] *Marmion*, Canto VI, Stanza 17. Sir Walter Scott (1771–1832) was a Scottish novelist, poet, historian.

may help us deal with the past to be able to put it to rest. Al-Anon can fill the same bill. Bringing up events and our memories of them and handling them can break the hold of the dark demons, bringing them into the light. The dreadful demons get smaller and we get bigger. We may feel less isolated when we hear others sharing similar experiences. Eventually we may have the joy of helping others by sharing our secrets in meetings.

When deciding to share some or all of our secrets, it is important to do so with people we can trust. We want someone who will keep our confidences and also be able to stick with us, even after hearing our dark secrets. We don't want everybody to know them. Not everybody is able to understand. For most of us, it is best to share them with someone familiar with the disease of alcoholism, at a meeting, or one-on-one with a trusted friend from the program. It would be rare indeed to have a secret no one else has dealt with. We are encouraged to remember that our Higher Power speaks through people, sometimes through us.

Secrecy can be one of the factors in the disease of alcoholism, which is often handed down from generation to generation. In the same way, recovery can be handed down. What a blessing to know that with us, the disease has stopped and the recovery has begun. Sharing is often the key to healing. If we can participate in the healthy sharing of our experiences and listening to the experiences of others, we may come to the place where we can risk being our true self with family members and letting them be their true selves.

Part of our quest for a healthy life may involve admitting we are not perfect. We are human and we make mistakes. It seems easier—and many of us have become comfortable with it—to justify an action or rationalize our reasons for behaving as we have, instead of acknowledging an error and apologizing or attempting to correct it. In admitting an error, we are taking responsibility for ourselves and we free ourselves from the burden of an embarrassing secret.

In this area, as everywhere, with the help of our Higher Power, we can have wisdom, discernment, and common sense.

<⊲ ☺ ⊳>

CAT DIARY

Day 983 of my captivity.

My captors continue to taunt me with bizarre little dangling objects.

They dine lavishly on fresh meat, while the other inmates and I are fed hash or some sort of dry nuggets.

Although I make my contempt for the rations perfectly clear, I nevertheless must eat something in order to keep up my strength.

The only thing that keeps me going is my dream of escape.

In an attempt to disgust them, I once vomited on the carpet.

Today I decapitated a mouse and dropped its headless body at their feet. I had hoped this would strike fear in their hearts, since it clearly demonstrates what I am capable of. However, they merely made condescending comments about what a good little hunter I am.

Today I was almost successful in an attempt to assassinate one of my tormentors by weaving around his feet while he was walking. I must try again tomorrow, but at the top of the stairs.

I am convinced that the other prisoners here are flunkies and snitches.

The dog gets special privileges. He is regularly released and seems to be more than willing to return. He is obviously mentally challenged.

The bird has got to be an informant. I observe him communicating with the guards regularly. I am certain he reports my every move.

My captors have arranged protective custody for him in an elevated cell, so he is safe...for now.

Cats still rule!!!

Remember Your Freedom

I have sworn upon the altar of God, eternal hostility against every form of tyranny over the mind of man.
Thomas Jefferson, inscribed on the Jefferson Memorial, Washington, D.C.

Ol' Tom wasn't thinking of addiction there, but his words apply. "It's a free country, I can do what I want." "It's my right to smoke." "I'm free to drink if I want." Have you ever heard young—or not so young—people say that? Have you said it yourself?

Of course, we are free to enjoy whatever behavior we wish to indulge in; we are also free to enjoy the consequences of behavior. Sometimes these consequences make us less than free. How free are we when we wake up in a strange bed—or on the floor of the Public Safety Building with half our teeth missing—and have no idea how we got there? Maybe total freedom isn't as free as we thought.

Perhaps we are freer when we confine our behavior to what is legal. James Dillet Freeman[42] was a 20th century American poet, the only one whose work was carried by two different astronauts when they landed on the moon. Freeman wrote an article on freedom for the American Bicentennial in July of 1976. It is the best we have ever seen. We are grateful to have permission to copy the article as it appeared in its entirety in the *Daily Word* magazine. It's called: "Of Freedom and Fences."[43]

---

[42] James Dillet Freeman (1912–2003), called the "modern-day Ralph Waldo Emerson," wrote many books and articles and served in various capacities in Unity School for over fifty years.
[43] Copied by permission of Unity School.

FREEDOM! The word rings like a bell, doesn't it? It lifts the heart and stirs the passions. But just what is freedom? How free can anyone be?

I have a dog, a saluki, a large, beautiful, extremely active dog. I live in a house with a large yard, almost a couple of acres. My dog has free access to the yard at all times through her own swinging door, and in house and yard she lives a very free life, for the most part doing only what she wants to do, as my wife and I make few demands on her, probably fewer than she makes on us. She flies from one end of the yard to the other, chasing anything that happens to be going by on the street, or any squirrel, cat, rabbit, or bird that ventures into the yard and she takes it into her head to chase.

My yard is fenced, but much of it is not a high fence, mainly ornamental. The fence is more a mental limit than a physical obstacle. Any time she wished she could be over it like the wind and off across the city. Not the fence, but only her own acceptance of the fence keeps her in the yard.

My dog and her fence have made me think about what freedom really is in very different terms than I had ever thought about it before. I have come to realize that the fence does not keep her in bondage, it keeps her free.

For suppose she did jump the fence and go wandering off? Would she be free? Freer than she now is? Out in the streets is a world of laws against unleashed dogs, angry neighbors, unfriendly dogs, dogcatchers, and speeding cars. How free would she be skittering frightened and bewildered through the unfamiliar maze of the city's streets? Have you ever seen a lost dog?

In the world that lies beyond the fence, there is no way she could remain free for long, at best, she would be taken into the house of some kind person; at worst, she would be locked up in the dog pound or even run over. The fence does not limit her freedom as much as it guarantees it. On the contrary, it marks how far she can go and not lose her freedom—relative freedom, it is true, but which of us has any other kind?

What limits my dog's freedom is not that fence, but the fact that she is a saluki who has to live in Lee's Summit, Missouri, U.S.A. on the continent of North America and the Planet Earth, in 1976. Similar limitations determine the freedom of us all.

95

Freedom is and always must be a relative matter. If I am wise, I do not insist on flying just because I would like to have wings. I walk when I have to. I may be free to step out of a window, but the moment I do, I lose my freedom. I am made captive and plummeted to earth by forces over which I have no control. I have asserted my freedom beyond my power to maintain it. I have gone beyond my fence.

I built my dog's fence. In the case of human beings, they themselves may have to build their fences. Not all, of course. Many of our fences have been built by wise and loving people who lived before us, examined the world—as I have for my dog—and realized where fences were needed if they were to preserve, and not lose, their liberty. If we are wise, we accept the fences raised for us by laws, by tradition, by religious belief, by the moral code, by good manners and consideration.

For if we go too far beyond the fences of reasonable restraint, we may find we have not extended our freedom, we have lost what freedom we had. To go too far is to come up short.

I wonder if we as a nation are still here after two hundred years because the founding fathers were as aware of fences as they were of freedom when they wrote the Declaration of Independence? For they set up a very fenced-in freedom, but it was one within which they could unite to get the country started, and within which we have been able—in spite of all the persisting inequities—to be the freest people the human race has so far managed to produce.

In our time many people insist on acting is if there are no fences. "I must be free!" they assert, and they think this means they have the right to act, say, or think as they please.

You have only to think about it to see that if everyone were free to do whatever he wished to do, it would result, not in freedom but in chaos. The world would be a hodgepodge, impossible work of infinite whim.

We are created to be free. The newborn child becomes enraged if you pinion him, and we never happily submit to domination, even our own. We are not puppets, no, not even God's! He made us to be free, for He made us in His image. That is why in the heart of every person stirs the desire freely to express his God-potential. That is why we feel this discontent with anything less than freedom. But we misinterpret it when we feel that it tells us throw off every restraint, every limitation.

There are two kinds of freedom in the world. We have to be free from and free to. But sometimes we try to be free from what we should be free to and free to what we should be free from. Then, in the name of freedom, we enslave ourselves.

For to be free means to be free from everything that keeps us from achieving our maximum potential; everything that weakens us; everything that tends to make us less than the most we are capable of being. And it means to be free to grow, to achieve dominion over our self and all the forces at work in us, to develop and express our creative powers.

The freedom that is God's free child's is not an easy freedom. It comes only with growth. It comes only with strength. It comes only with the power to stand firm. It comes only with mastery. And mastery comes only out of discipline.

Without discipline there is no freedom. My dog has helped me to learn this, too. For us to enjoy a free walk together on a country afternoon, she must have learned to heel, come, and stay when I tell her to. When she was a puppy, we both went to obedience school and there I learned that if I was to become the master, I had first to master myself. Getting her to obey was not hard once I had learned to obey. Her discipline depended almost entirely on how disciplined I was. We are, all of us, freest when we have the maximum control over ourselves and our life, when we can say to ourselves, "Go!" and we may go when we can say, "Stay!" and we stay.

The undisciplined life, the unrestrained life, is not the freest life; it is the least free. The undisciplined are imprisoned by their own lack of strength and skill. Instead of mounting on their limitations and learning to ride them to triumph, they let their limitations ride them.

The skater flying across the ice, how effortlessly she weaves through what fantastic patterns! The musician improvising at the piano, how freely his spirit ranges over the keys, fountains of music cascading from his fingertips! The basketball player, how carelessly he flicks the ball over his shoulder that it should fall so cleanly through the net! And the football player, with what unpremeditated art he spins through the field of tacklers!

How free! How beautiful! We exclaim. But we know that this beautiful freedom can come only after how many months, how many years of the hardest, most persistent practice. The power to be free had to be first of all the will to submit.

Where there are no fences, there is no freedom. Not for long. Sometimes I think no one must know the meaning of the value of freedom better than the man or woman in Alcoholics Anonymous. They have met their challenge and made it their conquest. They have taken the measure of their limitations, and made it the measure of their freedom. They have learned how to live freely—within their fences. The peaks of freedom never have been scaled except by those who had the courage and the will to submit to the necessities of the endeavor.

"Where the Spirit of the Lord is, there is liberty." And the Spirit of the Lord is wisdom, is strength, is self-control. Even more, it is control by the highest forces and highest elements in our being.

You should never have your best trousers on when you go out to fight for freedom and truth.
Attributed to Henrik Ibsen

If you don't change directions, you could end up where you're headed.
In a fortune cookie

Long ago, when men cursed and beat the ground with sticks, it was called witchcraft. Today it's called golf.
Attributed to Will Rogers

Being Willing

When we least expect it, life sets us a challenge to test
our courage and willingness to change.
Paulo Cuelho[44]

~

Suppose we find occasional water spots on our kitchen floor. No big deal. Then the spots become larger and seem to coincide with rain. Someone suggests the problem could be a leaky roof. Well, maybe, but we don't think so. Then a typhoon-sized rainstorm comes, and we see drops and then cups and finally buckets of water come through the roof and make pools on the kitchen floor.

At last, we can deny the problem no longer. We do, indeed, have a leaky roof. We are no longer in denial. Does this mean our problem is gone? Hardly! The leaky roof will not improve—it can only get worse—until we decide to do something about it. We must be willing to call the roofing professional, our cousin who has put on a couple of roofs, our good buddies who've said, "Call me anytime you need anything." Getting the roof fixed, after we have decided there is a problem, takes willingness on our part to do something. And so it is with any change. We must be willing to stop what we've been doing—denying the problem of the leaky roof—and take some action, even if it's only looking up some numbers in the phonebook.

A recovering alcoholic relates:

I first knew Billy and Jim all the way back in Jr. High School. Billy was an athlete, one of the local jocks that played most sports. Basketball was his favorite, and since it was also

---
[44] Paulo Cuelho (b. 1947), Brazilian lyricist and novelist.

mine, we often found ourselves on the same court. Jimmy, on the other hand, was more of a social animal, found on the party circuit. He knew his way around the local bars by the time he was a high school junior. So did I.

After high school, I saw little of them as I was off to college, a stint in the army, marriage and a family. I was also perfecting my alcoholism. Eventually, I returned to one of the old familiar watering holes, and became re-acquainted with Billy and Jim. We remained "buddies" for many years, till death did us part. Over twenty years ago, I got into recovery, but I still stopped into the bar in the mornings to have a cup of coffee with my old buddies.

Billy was now manager of the pub and later became the owner of his own watering hole. When I became sober, Billy acknowledged that he drank too much and was probably an alcoholic. He did not consider it a great handicap, since booze was his livelihood. So being alcoholic was acceptable to his lifestyle and work. Of course the atmosphere was full of smoke and Bill enjoyed this habit, too. I lost Billy as a friend last year to lung cancer. He had never been willing to change, even though he recognized his alcohol and smoking addictions and knew they were not healthy.

Jimmy was a traveling salesman, or so he claimed from his bar stool. He spent a good part of every day in the local pub, but every two weeks or so he would tell us how he was going on the road selling his wares. Jim would not show up for a few days, but his car was often spotted near another pub in a more distant part of the city during these "road trips." Jimmy would often tell me how much he admired my sobriety and "willpower," and wished he could stop. He never said he was an alcoholic, but the insinuation was there and his wife used the term freely when talking about him. His appearance had been growing puffy and reddish for several years, and it was easy to see the physical deterioration that was happening to him. When we came back from our last vacation, I ran into his wife, who told me of his passing. She remarked how much she wished he had followed my example twenty years ago. He knew he had a problem, but he was unwilling to even try to fix it.

Both of my friends lacked the willingness that could have made recovery possible and probably lengthened and improved the quality of their lives. Let's face it, there is not much quality in sitting on a bar stool looking at brown bottles and talking about who is the best team and how we would run the world from our stools.

It is easy to see how unwillingness to change keeps alcoholics from sobriety. But what about us? Does this apply to those of us who live or work or deal with alcoholics? A co-dependent relates:

> I had gotten over the denial of my husband's alcohol problem, although I wouldn't discuss it with anyone. A friend suggested Al-Anon might be useful to me. I did give it some thought—very little, to be sure. I was simply not ready to do anything. Not WILLING might be a better description. I was absolutely unwilling to put myself out, certainly not until the alcoholic made a move in the right direction. Thankfully, he did eventually get to a rehab, and at their suggestion, I tried Al-Anon. Looking back I wonder if my husband might have found sobriety sooner if I had gone to Al-Anon sooner. At the very least, my life would've been happier if I had been willing to try.

A person who has the serenity of the program might say: "If you want what I have, you must be WILLING to learn what I learned and make the changes I made!"

◁ ☺ ▷
OBSERVATIONS

Dolphins are so smart that within a few weeks of captivity, they can train people to stand on the very edge of the pool and throw them fish.

I thought I wanted a career; turns out I just wanted paychecks.

A bank is a place that will lend you money, but only if you can prove that you don't need it.

Whenever I fill out an application, in the part that says "If an emergency, notify:" I put DOCTOR.

I didn't say it was your fault. I said I was blaming you.

Why does someone believe you when you say there are four billion stars but check when you say the paint is wet?

Why do Americans choose from just two people to run for President and fifty for Miss America?

Stinkin' Thinkin'

*Whether you think you can or think you can't,
either way you are right.
Henry Ford*[45]

People in AA sometimes refer to stinkin' thinkin.' What is that? Thinking in a negative, fruitless way. Is it good for us? What do you think?

Many, perhaps most of us, brought up in addicted or otherwise dysfunctional families learned the practice of negative thinking. Blame. Gossip. Seeing the world as an unpleasant, nasty place. Expecting the worst. Expecting something terrible to happen, which happened often enough to justify the expectation. And if it didn't, we were pleasantly surprised.

What's the opposite of stinkin' thinkin'? Thinking that is positive, joyful, high, and hopeful might be its opposite. Might it have a beneficial effect on us? Would it be worth a try?

Even so, it is not easy to make the change to such a different way of thinking, and it's not only because the media—and those around us—trumpet all the negatives there are and even add a few. We are not comfortable with this new way of thinking.

We are accustomed to our Eeyore persona. You remember Eeyore in Milne's[46] classic, *Winnie the Pooh*: "Good morning, Pooh Bear, if it is a good morning, which I doubt."

So many of us in the alcoholic family scene have been in victim mode for a very long time. We are used to it. There is a comfort in

---

[45] Henry Ford (1863–1947), American industrialist, founder of the Ford Motor Company, inventor of mass production.
[46] AA Milne (1882–1956), English author, best known for *Winnie the Pooh*.

the familiar. It's not much different from getting a new pair of shoes. The old ones may be shredding and taking water on wet days, but a new pair has to be broken in before it feels right. Awful as it may be, we are comfortable in our gloom and doom and self-pity and don't want to give up our victim role.

Could there be something better? Could we just entertain the thought of progressing from Victim to Survivor? There are people who have survived horrendous situations: devastating events, terrible disease, being prisoners of war. Many of them have said that the turning point came when they stopped saying: "God, why me?" Instead, they began saying: "God, what am I to learn from this? What do you want me to do with this situation?"

For sixty-nine days in the late summer of 2010, people around the world were glued to their TV sets, watching what was happening to thirty-three Chilean miners trapped underground. Their survival and rescue provided the brightest spot in a year filled with conflict, recession, corruption, misunderstanding—you remember. These miners survived and came through. How did they do it?

An Everest climber and survival expert, Bear Grylls,[47] said the way to survival is:

- Be positive,
- Be inventive, and
- Never give up.

The miners seem to have practiced these ideas. The miners had each other and their families for comfort and strength as well as the thoughts and prayers of people around the world.

What do we have? We have the ability to be positive, inventive, and to never give up. We also have the support of those who, like us, are struggling with the effects of addiction and those who have managed to survive and thrive—those in our recovery programs.

The miners were not instantly at the surface. It took a while for each to emerge wearing thick black glasses. For us, it also takes a while. It's something like the end of a long, cold northern winter. One day the air is different and tiny green shoots are appearing. There will be more cold, more snow, maybe even a blizzard or two, but we have turned the corner on winter. In much the same way, one day we realize that the mental air is lighter and fresher, and that even though there will be storms again, we have turned the corner on stinkin' thinkin.'

---

[47] Bear Grylls (b. 1974), British adventurer, writer, TV presenter, youngest Englishman to climb Mt. Everest.

◁ ☺ ▷
MORE OBSERVATIONS

In the '60s, people took acid to make the world weird. Now the world is weird and people take Prozac to make it normal.

How is it that one careless match can start a forest fire, but it takes a whole box to start a campfire?

Who was the first person to look at a cow and say, "I think I'll squeeze these dangly things here and drink whatever comes out?"

If Jimmy cracks corn and no one cares, why is there a song about him?

Have a Bit of Humor—
The Good Kind

It's only truly funny if everyone can laugh!

∼

In 1979, Christine Clifford, a cancer patient, reflected that for the past six months people had been very kind to her, sending cards, books, food, flowers, everything, but there was something missing. She realized that, in all that time, no one had made her laugh. So she wrote a little book, *Not Now...I'm Having a No Hair Day*, dealing with the funny side of cancer, chemo, etc.[48]

A few decades earlier, Norman Cousins, an editor, contracted a painful disease of the connective tissues, from which only one in 500 patients ever recovers. Cousins was not ready to die and believed that the hospital and his treatments were not helping him. With his doctor's blessing, he checked out of the hospital and into a hotel.

Having ample funds and contacts in the entertainment industry, he got a movie projector set up in his room and his favorite shows brought in—this was before VHS tapes and DVDs. He loved movies of the Marx Brothers and re-runs of "Candid Camera." Cousins discovered that a half-hour of deep belly laughs could give him two hours of pain-free sleep.

Cousins made a complete recovery and wrote a book about his experience entitled *Anatomy of an Illness as Perceived by the*

---

[48] Christine Clifford, *Not Now...I'm Having a No Hair Day* (Minneapolis: University of Minnesota Press, 1996).

Patient.[49] He, an editor by education and profession, spent the last years of his life on the faculty of UCLA's medical school. Maybe he was on to something.

Is humor useful for other stressful situations? I once heard it said that during the Civil War a woman irately lambasted Abraham Lincoln for laughing and joking while the nation was in the worst crisis of its existence. Lincoln looked at her and said, "Madam, if I did not laugh, I would surely die."

Here's the experience of a friend:

When I was in 6th grade, my friend and I helped Mrs. Matthews, the kindergarten teacher. She was out for several months, dealing with the illness and death of her husband and returned the day before Christmas vacation. In our class, we'd had a gift exchange and I got a jar of jam—what a crummy present, but I took off the lid and voila! A big green snake jumped out.

I didn't know if I should show the present to Mrs. Matthews. After all, death is such a serious thing. I got nervy and handed her the jar. She opened it, the snake jumped out and she got a horrified look on her face, then burst out laughing. She hugged me and said, "Oh, thank you, that's the first laugh I've had in months."

After high school, I had bone surgery that was quite painful. One Sunday afternoon, a family stopped to see me after church. They were the funniest family I knew and kept me laughing with tales of the minister and his faux pas, as well as the little brats and teenagers acting up in the service. When they left, I happened to glance at the clock and realized forty-five minutes had gone by and I had felt no pain.

Later, I read *Anatomy of an Illness* and began to understand the healing power of humor.

Years ago, some alcoholics were setting down guidelines for their fellowship when a fellow noticed how glum they looked. He came up with a good thought: "Don't take yourself too damn seriously."

One might wonder if the words humor, human, and humility could possibly have the same root. Humor makes it easier to deal with the human condition; the ability to laugh, especially at ourselves, can wipe out our pretensions and give us a humility that can endear us to others.

---

[49] Norman Cousins, *Anatomy of an Illness as Perceived by the Patient* (New York: W. W. Norton and Company, 2001).

One word of caution: certain types of humor can be a defense weapon used to protect us from attacks by the stressful people in our lives. It can be used to attack others who we feel are not doing right by us. Some of us have used nasty humor (sarcasm) to make others look bad and ourselves look good. The root word of sarcasm is a Greek word meaning "to tear flesh." Is this what we REALLY want? Unless we're going for political comedy or satire, it's probably in our best interest to use more gentle humor. Did your parent or teacher ever say, "Unless everyone can laugh, it's not funny"?

Humor can be useful in situations where one wants to communicate something without offending another person. Here's a poem written by the cleaning lady to a kindergarten teacher who was not too careful about what was going on in her bathroom:

My dear Mrs. Johnson, I implore
You to rid me of who's peeing the floor,
It's been much more than a week,
And I just have to speak,
And hope you can settle the score.
My dear Mrs. Johnson, what's this?
Why should the porcelain be missed?
They better watch where they sprinkle
When they start to tinkle,
Or else I am going to get—mad.

An eminent psychiatrist once said that in his forty-some years of practice, he had seen very few patients who had a well-developed sense of the ridiculous. Furthermore, in all that time, he had NEVER been called upon to treat a person who could truly laugh at himself or herself! WOW!!

So humor is good. What if I don't feel like laughing? What if I can't see anything funny? A woman in recovery said she had been in the program about ten years and was just developing a sense of humor. Her sense of humor was extremely valuable to her, right up there with her serenity. Could this mean we can work at developing humor the same way we would develop any trait or skill?

No two people like exactly the same things—food, movies, vacation spots, etc. Humor is also an individual thing. You may not laugh at what your teenager thinks is funny. You may laugh at the boss's joke without seeing anything funny about it, but the boss is the boss and it makes sense to give a courtesy laugh.

How do you know what you like if you've never been into humor? Why not try an experiment? Dip into various kinds of humor and see what appeals to you. There is no right or wrong here; it is a matter of personal preference. Some folks love slapstick like Abbott and Costello or the Marx Brothers or the Three Stooges. Others prefer their humor more subtle, liking Bob Hope or George Burns. Some go for the "in-between" of Benny Hill, Bill Cosby, Lucile Ball, or Carol Burnett. Some like one-liners, others like a story line. It is up to you. You might peruse the comedy section of the video store and rent a few different vids to see what appeals to you. Or go to the bookstore or library and check out the humor section. Try the late late TV comedians and decide if any are worth staying up for. If so and you don't want to miss sleep, record the program.

If there is an open AA meeting in your area, you might find it an eye opener for more than one reason. Many of us are surprised that in these meetings, people share horror stories of what has happened to them as a result of their addiction. But there is often a lot of laughter going on, too. Amazing how people with so little to laugh about can laugh so much!

Once you have an idea of what jabs your funny bone, you could set aside a bit of time each day to practice laughing—which someone recently said was awfully good for the abdominal muscles. Can hearty laughter give you great abs? Maybe yes, maybe no. It's worth a try and has only beneficial side effects.

◁☺▷
PUNS FOR THE EDUCATED MINDS

1. A vulture boards an airplane, carrying two dead raccoons. The stewardess looks at him and says, "I'm sorry, sir, only one carrion allowed per passenger."
2. No matter how much you push the envelope, it'll still be stationery.
3. Two silk worms had a race. They ended up in a tie.
4. Time flies like an arrow. Fruit flies like a banana.
5. Atheism is a non-prophet organization.
6. Two hats were hanging on a hat rack in the hallway. One hat said to the other, "You stay here, I'll go on a head."
7. I wondered why the baseball kept getting bigger. Then it hit me.
8. The midget fortune-teller who escaped from prison was a small medium at large.
9. A backward poet writes inverse.
10. If you jumped off the bridge in Paris, you'd be in Seine.

The Importance of Humility

Refrain therefore awhile from setting yourself up
as a judge of the highest matters.
Plato[50]

Humility is NOT humiliation. Humility is NOT being a doormat. Humility is NOT giving someone else power to control your life. Humility is NOT always putting the wants and needs of others above your own. Humility is NOT weakness. So if humility ISN'T these things, what IS humility and what can it do?

Maybe the highest form of humility is the ability to see yourself with a true perspective, to perceive your true relationship with your Higher Power and with your fellow human beings, to say, "I'm as good as you are, you're as good as I am, and God is infinitely better than both of us."

Humility can wipe out obstacles to your true self. It can help you set your world in order by changing your thinking. (Remember, if you change the way you look at things, the things you look at change. Remember that the glass can be half-full or half-empty.)

Humility is being teachable, moldable, and receptive. It helps you open your mind so you can learn from every person and situation. It helps you accept the good in everyone and avoid personal judgments. It enables you to take ideas from everyone and to not judge by appearances—like raggedy clothes, bad grammar, station

---

[50] Al-Anon, *Courage to Change* (Al-Anon Family Group Headquarters, 1992), 225.

109

in life. It reminds you that you don't have all the answers—or even all the questions. It can aid your recovery.

What is the opposite of humility? There are several opposites. There is pride, not pride in the sense of self-esteem, but pride in the sense of feeling better than someone else. Arrogance is pride to the nth degree. Self-will is also the opposite of humility. When you are hung up in self-will, you are pushing out God's will even though God's will is much better for you. A friend in an Al-Anon meeting noted that "EGO" is Edging God Out.

Have you ever looked at someone and thought of the person as being below you? Most of us have. We can see people who are not as good-looking, brainy, talented as we are. But if we look at people this way, we have to see that there are people more good-looking, brainy, talented. We are perpetually on a ladder, with others both above and below us. We might consider getting off the ladder of judgment to take our rightful place on par with everyone else. One friend relates that, as she was mentally berating someone, her Higher Power clearly said, "Who the hell made you the judge?" Another friend mentions needing to pray often: "God, help me climb down off my high horse before I get knocked off." Humility helps us avoid the need to worry about such things. It can help us practice love and tolerance toward all—including ourselves.

Humility helps us get ready to surrender. What?! Surrender? That's giving up. That's not what I want. I need to take care of myself. I need to take charge of my responsibilities. What's this surrender stuff, anyhow?

Just wait. Surrender does NOT mean submission. It means you're willing to stop fighting reality. It means you stop trying to do God's job. Surrender is acknowledging you are not in control (have we heard this before?) and that you can and must let your Higher Power take care of the world, your loved ones, AND you. You turn your fear and your love over to your Higher Power.

We've heard of the 12 Steps. Step 7 states that we HUMBLY ask God to remove our defects of character. If we are unable to be humble, it's doubtful God can do much to remove our character defects. In fact, if we are really "unhumble," we may be unable to recognize such a defect, even if it bites us on the butt!

Humility is one of the most useful virtues. Yeah?? Yeah!! It enhances our relationships with others. A humble person is a non-threatening person. We don't get our hackles up and try to push back on someone who doesn't push on us. Fellow workers are much more apt to help and make allowances for a person they don't see as a threat. Humble people are good team players; they allow everyone to get credit for successes.

Sometimes we find good sayings on placemats, napkins, etc. Here's one from a calendar: "Humility truly is the mother of all virtues. It makes us a vessel, a vehicle, an agent instead of 'the source' or the principal. It unleashes all other learning, all growth and process."[51]

We humbly submit these ideas for your consideration and contemplation with an eye to the Higher Power of us all.

If you are all wrapped up in yourself, you are overdressed.
Kate Halverson[52]

Never eat more than you can lift.
Miss Piggy[53]

---

[51] *First Things First* calendar for August 7, 1997.
[52] Helen Nash and Dorothy Masterson, *Humorous Cryptograms* (Sterling, 1995).
[53] Sharon Tyler Herbst, Never Eat More Than You Can Lift and Other Food Quotes and Quips (Broadway, 1997).

How to Accept Being Powerless Over People, Places, and Things

Sure you're powerless...sure you can't change anything, but you don't have to be miserable about it as well.
Lydia Lunch[54]

∾

"If he really loved me, he would stop drinking."
"When we are married, I will fix him/her."
"If only I were a better daughter/son, they wouldn't drink/drug."
"If only I were a better housekeeper, smarter, thinner, fatter, better looking, more understanding, a better husband, wife, mother, father, etc., etc., etc."

Any of these sound familiar? If not, there are more. All show how powerless we are in terms of controlling another person's actions. No matter how hard we try, we cannot make someone else do something. We can plead, beg, cajole, threaten, or make it illegal and still people do what they will do. Even the shadow of the death penalty doesn't keep people from killing each other. Do we have anything that strong in our bag of threats?

Some philosophers and theologians argue for predestination, that all events have been willed by God. Some psychologists say everything we do is a necessary result of past experiences and we have no real choice in our actions. Either thought makes whatever we do seem meaningless. It also works toward the idea of powerlessness. But, as one fellow says: "In my experience as a counselor

---

[54] Lydia Lunch (b. Lydia Koch, 1959), American singer, poet, writer, actress.

and recovering addict, I find this goes against what I have seen and my own gut instinct." But the idea does illustrate powerlessness.

Just try to control something. Can we control the weather, what someone says to us, whether or not the bus is on time today, or whether or not Congress declares war? What it boils down to is that we can only control what we, ourselves, do—and even then, with limitations. For instance, have we said the wrong thing because we put our foot in our mouth before our brain was in gear? Or did we repeat something to someone, only to find the person was the town gossip? O did we give someone an idea that he used and took credit for? So if we can't control our own words and their results, we can hardly expect to control someone else's.

Try to control someone. Start with a little baby. The baby is crying and you want him to stop. You rock him and that lasts for a minute and he starts again. Aha! It's bottle time. You give the little darling a bottle, he starts sucking, and all is well. You made him stop crying, didn't you? Really? The little tyke stopped because he wanted to eat and chow was served. It was under his control all the time. He could and would have continued crying if he'd had an upset stomach instead of hunger. You were not in control.

He has grown up a bit and now plays with the other kids on the block. You try to watch out for him and tell him all the *don't*s you can think of. Then one day he comes crying down the street with blood streaming from his head. You fear he has been shot. You run and find out he has a cut where he was hit by a stone thrown by another kid. It was a game and they were all participating, including your little dear. He should have known better, you had told him a million times...

As the years go by, you teach him the evils of smoking, alcohol, drugs, and casual sex and are outraged to find that he has done them all on his way to adulthood.

To put it simply, we do not have control or power over what someone else does; we can try to be an influence for good (or bad), but that is where our control ends. We are often out of control ourselves, but with work, we can do something about that.

Finally, by recognizing that we are powerless over others, especially those we have always believed we should be able to control, we can free ourselves from feelings of guilt over their actions. It is a great relief to know we are not responsible for the world but only for ourselves.

The old statement "Do the best you can with what you've got" is a key to serenity and acceptance of our true place in the world.

◁ ☺ ▷

I just got off the phone with one of my friends in northeast Nebraska. He said that it has been snowing since early this morning and that the snow is nearly waist-high and is still falling. The temperature is dropping below zero and the north wind is increasing. His wife has done nothing but look through the kitchen window. He says that if it gets much worse, he may have to let her in.

Avoid the Enabler

God helps those who help themselves.
From the Bible? Wrong. Probably the most quoted phrase
NOT found in the Bible.[55]

~

The enabler is not exactly a rare animal. In fact, they are all around us. Are they useful? Sometimes yes and sometimes no. Our churches, universities, charitable institutions, etc., could not function without the work and/or financial backing of many ordinary people. They are enabling this work to be done.

Many people—in fact, most people—are enablers. When someone helps us along on some goal or project, that person is being an enabler by helping us do something. This could be sending us to a friend who has a job opening that might suit us. This would normally be considered a good thing since referrals are the best way to find a good job. Should the job turn out to be a real dog, however, we might consider it a bad thing and, while the intentions of the enabler were very good, the result may have been disastrous because we took the wrong job. So what we have is a person who, with good intentions but a probable lack of knowledge, has not helped us at all but may have caused some harm. As the old saying goes, "the road to hell is paved with good intentions."

So, for all practical purposes, an enabler is someone who is trying to help by easing the way for someone else. The intentions are laudable, but the results don't necessarily follow the desires of the helper. IN THE CASE OF ENABLERS INVOLVED WITH ALCOHOL OR OTHER DRUG ABUSERS, THE ENABLING IS ALMOST ALWAYS CONSIDERED THE WRONG ACTION. Consider these examples:

---

[55] Attributed to Ben Franklin in *Poor Richard's Almanac*. Originally attributed to Sydney Algernon (1622–1683).

Jack drinks too much and his parents know it, but they hope it is only a "phase he is going through." Jack gets a DWI (Driving While Intoxicated) ticket. His parents are feeling very indignant toward the police and the system for picking on their child. They hire the best lawyer they can and try to get him off.

Richie is a fine young student athlete. His father and coach both feel he could be a superstar but could use some additional size and strength. It seems that Richie has found a supply of anabolic steroids. No one is looking too closely.

Craig wakes up on another Monday morning with a big hangover. His wife, Monica, has called in sick for him. "He has such a bad cold...he just isn't up to working today." Craig is sleeping it off on the couch. This is not the first time Monica has called in sick for Craig.

Leonard is at the bar, too plastered to even walk home, let alone drive the car. The bartender (who knows Len well after his many visits to this bar) calls his house and one of the older kids walks over to fetch his good old dad and the family car.

A great example that shows all of the bad things about enabling is the classic bounced check, another episode with Craig and Monica. Our abuser needs more money for his drug of choice (a couple of six packs and some cash to spend at the local pub), so he cashes a check at the store, but there is not enough money in the bank account to cover it. Monica does not want the family to be embarrassed by having a check bounce at the local grocery store. So she borrows money from her mom and dad without telling them the real reason she needs it. Now the wife is angry and resentful over this situation. She lets Craig know her feelings one way or another. He, in turn, is resentful of his wife and her attitude. This is just one more reason for him to go out and drink (or drug) because she is the reason he does it in the first place. Does this sound familiar to anyone? Even without the wife, who wouldn't drink with kids like Craig's? But beyond the feelings that are unleashed, he has managed to get away with something without any penalty. So guess what Craig is going to do the next time he needs some cash? He has learned that the family will take care of it. Good lesson learned, isn't it? This is enabling at its best—or worst.

What have we lost here? Let's check Monica first. She has enabled her mate by paying off his overdrawn check. To be sure, saving the family the embarrassment of a bounced check does not seem to be a bad thing by itself. Most of us would probably go to extremes to avoid the embarrassment of apologizing and making amends for this kind of error. However, Monica has still suffered the humbling embarrassment of having to borrow money from her parents. They are not dumb, and they probably have some idea that the need is associated with their son-in-law's drinking. They may already have developed some animosity toward him. Given enough time, they may even feel she should leave him. At the very least, some strain has developed in this part of the family. Monica has also developed some stress about her dealings with her family and another bit of stress over how to pay her parents back. And let's not forget the guilt of lying to her parents, even when she suspects they probably know the truth. Now she must face the future knowing a similar situation could happen again at any time.

Craig has also learned something. He has a family that will rescue him from his financial woes. When he makes a mistake, someone will bail him out without interfering with his drinking. Of course he has a great deal of guilt that needs to be buried. The easy way to deal with his own unacceptable feelings is to divert them from himself to the people closest to him. After all, who else would you dump on except those who love you and are loyal to you? But worst of all, Craig has lost a chance to grow. When we experience adversity, we have the opportunity to learn and grow. Facing the consequences of his actions might have given Craig this opportunity, now derailed by the enablers in his life.

Going back to some of the earlier examples, let's look at Jack and his parents. The first thing we encounter is the denial that this DWI is anything but a mistake of youth that will not happen again. The parents are blaming the police and the system and just plain bad luck, not Jack's behavior. In truth, people are seldom picked up for DWI. If they do get picked up, it is probably the odds of many occurrences catching up with them. At any rate, Jack has broken the law and his parents are treating it like a raid on the cookie jar, making it easier for Jack to continue his drinking and driving. Luckily, the justice system will probably make it a little harder for Jack to continue his harmful and illegal behavior. It may, at least, keep him more aware and perhaps he will use a cab or designated driver sometimes. Perhaps!

There is so much emphasis on winning in sports that many young athletes, along with their coaches and peers, seem all too willing to turn to the use of anabolic steroids or anything else that will enhance the athlete's performance. Anabolic steroids do add muscle and size to youth that have not yet closed their growth plates. Most people are aware that anabolic steroids do enhance performance in sports, but they are not fully aware of the side effects they have, or they are willing to sacrifice future health for the fame and/or fortune that may come with their use. In Richie's case, we have both a coach looking for team success and a dad looking for his son's success, with either the coach or the dad aiding and abetting steroid use.

In general, steroids differ from other drugs in that they are not used for their mind-altering effects; therefore, some people like to fool themselves into thinking they are not as bad as other drugs. The long-term effects on the body are severe, and the enablers are helping the youth to be dishonest as well as letting him suffer long-term adverse results. Even so, they think they are helping. The paving on the road to hell is popping up to smack us in the face.

Leonard is fortunate; the bartender is wise enough to not let Len drive. This is the most productive enabling we are seeing. The barkeep has kept Len from a potential accident, but on the other side of the coin, he has allowed Len to drink far beyond the normal limits and needs to cover his own butt in case Len is stopped and tells where he got this overload of ethanol. Len has been bailed out again and knows he can get away with his excesses because some-one will save him. Once again, he has been enabled.

We have covered enabling from several angles, and in most cases when we deal with mind-altering drugs, the results are nega-tive. Enabling allows the abusers to continue on without facing the consequences of their behavior; the opportunity for positive growth is lost, as is any real attempt at intervention of the negative behavior. From the position of the enabler, the results are usually stressful and guilt-ridden with lies and deceptions, even though he or she had the best of intentions, intentions stemming from love. What a mess!!! And what is the cure? We must train ourselves to recognize this behavior before we act. We must decide what direction we are going to take and act upon it. Is this easy? HELL, NO!! And doing it by ourselves is nearly impossible.

Where do we get help if this is so difficult to recognize and act upon? Two major sources of help are available, and both have advantages. When used together they are best, but either by itself can work.

The first is counseling. The advantage to this is that it offers more concentrated help with you as a main focus. Both group and individual meetings are available. The disadvantages are high costs, limited time with the counselor, and sometimes inconvenient meeting places.

The second is the 12-Step programs. Al-Anon is a wonderful choice. The cost is a free-will donation, and there are many meetings in most major population areas. Everyone is there to help you and is also looking to you to help them. It is often easier to see possible solutions to a problem someone else is having than it is to see solutions to your own. The possible downsides of this source of help are inconvenient meeting places, inconvenient meeting times, and difficulties in trying to protect a professional status in a small community while attending face-to-face meetings.

Many of us have seen enabling and have been enablers from an early age. And it seemed the right thing to do. It won't be easy to change. It's a lot of work, but it is so worth it. Detachment is the key to making the change.

HOW TO DETACH

We see that enabling is very common and can be good, but in the case of addicted persons, it is not. Calling in sick for a spouse, or writing an excuse for a child who didn't get his science project done because he was stoned are, at best, short-term fixes and allow the addicted one to continue destructive, foolish, or inappropriate behavior that will only get worse. What can be done? We love these people. We only want them to be OK. The answer is to detach.

Does this mean that we should detach from our loved one and have nothing to do with him or her? It may, but usually we are advised to first detach from our own enabling behavior and allow our loved ones to experience the consequences of their actions without our interference. There are various ways to detach: *physically* by moving to another room—or another city; *mentally* by monitoring our thoughts and refusing to entertain thoughts of doing for loved ones what they could and should be doing for themselves; *emotionally* by not allowing ourselves to be sucked in by appeals to our sympathy or by threats of the terrible things that may happen if we don't bail the abuser out.

Detachment is a behavior for us. It can be done in different ways. Detaching with anger is relatively easy and is often our first reaction. Al-Anon speaks of detaching with love, which is far better in the long run.

"Know thyself." Before embarking on what will be, for most, a drastic change, it might be good to know where we stand. Why are we enabling? Is it out of habit, fear, the desire to cover up and look good, or something else? What are the positives and negatives of making the change to detachment? Like many other life changes, detachment may cause us a great deal of discomfort at first. But, remembering that the definition of insanity is doing the same thing over and over expecting different results, the ultimate result of learning to practice detachment may be a progression to a more sane and serene life.

My husband paid the bills. I was unsure as to what was going on but let it go. I handed him the phone with the bill collector on the other end. It was HIS responsibility. Then he died. I was surprised and shocked to learn of numerous unpaid bills and charges that were now MY responsibility.
Claire, Al-Anon member

We might want to protect our families and ourselves by being more aware of what is going on financially. By the same token, we might be wise to learn our legal responsibilities for our children, especially the teens.

Like a great many benefits in life, detachment needs work, but it is a behavior that, if practiced, will contribute to our peace of mind and well-being.

◁☺▷
QUESTIONS
1. Does a clean house indicate that there is a broken computer in it?
2. Is there ever a day that mattresses are *not* on sale?
3. Why do people constantly return to the refrigerator with hopes that something new to eat will have materialized?
4. Why do people keep running over a string a dozen times with their vacuum cleaner, then reach down, pick it up, examine it, then put it down to give the vacuum one more chance?
5. Why is it that no plastic garbage bag will open from the end you first try?
6. How do those dead bugs get into those closed light fixtures?
7. Why is it that whenever you attempt to catch something that's falling off the table, you always manage to knock something else over?
8. Is it true that the only difference between a yard sale and a trash pickup is how close to the road the stuff is placed?
9. In winter why do we try to keep the house as warm as it was in summer when we complained about the heat?
10. If at first you don't succeed, shouldn't you try doing it like your wife told you to do it?

How to Let Go
of Resentment

It ain't good for you.
Anonymous

Nothing on earth consumes a man [or a woman] more
quickly than the passion of resentment.
Friedrich Nietzsche[56]

Resentment affects most people at one time or another. Think back to childhood: when you did everything your mom asked, but she let your brother go to the circus and you had to stay home and help with the baby; when you wrote a good essay and another kid copied it, changed it just a bit, and got a better grade; when some bigger kids cut in front of you in the lunchroom and nobody did anything about it. Then in adolescence, your best friend stole your boyfriend, you had a great idea for the senior theme and someone else got the credit. Then you became an adult and nothing changed, the same sort of things happened again. And again...and again...

Those of us who grew up in addictive or otherwise dysfunctional homes (and remember, addicted families have no monopoly on dysfunction) may "catch" resentment like a cold. Or it might be better to say we learned it early on from those around us. Resentment may be a learned behavior, or it may just come naturally. It may be one way we learn to deal with anger—we are told that it is not nice to express anger, so we stuff it down, down, down and forget about it. But it doesn't go away and may come out as resentful, dissatisfied thoughts that may not be appropriate to our present situation.

---

[56] Friedrich Nietzsche, *Ecce Homo* (New York: Dover Publications, 2004), 21.

Goodness knows, living with an addicted spouse brings many opportunities for resentment. And if a child develops an addiction, along with the worry and fear, there is likely to be resentment toward the child and maybe toward other family members. Resentment is doubtless a natural and obvious way to deal with stuffed-down anger.

But is it good for us? Is it in our own best interest? You may remember back to the story of the woman whose husband promised to be home to take her out and showed up hours later, bombed out of his mind. She was justifiably angry and when the fellow passed out cold, unaware of her berating, her anger and resentment boiled over, shooting poison through her body. The tiny cold sore on her lip erupted into an angry festering lesion, leaving a scar that lasted many years until it had to be removed to avoid cancer.

Consider also the quote from Dorothy, who had spent her life with alcoholics, concerning her ulcer: "It's not what I'm eating … it's what's eating me!" It would be interesting to know how many cases of other gastro-intestinal disorders (colitis, diverticulitis, etc.) or skin conditions or migraines or life threatening diseases or even cancer have been caused, or at least exacerbated, by the practice of nursing deep-seated resentments.

So, who is our resentment hurting? The alcoholic or addict? Probably not. He or she has a powerful drug to blot out feelings of shame or inadequacy. So who is hurt? Could it be our children, as they ride the roller coaster of conflicting messages from the alcoholic AND us? "I love you/go away, I'm here for you/I'm outta here," and "Daddy has an illness and we need to be patient/your father is a bum." So our children are probably hurt and may develop stress-related illnesses themselves as they grow up sandwiched between the stresses of the alcoholic parent and the resentful parent.

In addition to our kids—and likely others we come in contact with—the bottom line is that we can be badly damaged by our own resentment. Is this what we want? Not really. What can we do? One thing might be to take ownership. It's OUR resentment, not anybody else's. It might be a good idea to search out our feelings and question exactly what we are resenting, what thoughts or feelings might be more productive than the resentment we are accustomed to. And then, we may need to acknowledge a need for help.

Think back to Step 1: we admitted we were powerless. Many of us realize we are powerless, not only over someone else's addiction but also over nearly everything else—including our own reflexes and feelings. Not a cheery situation. But remember Step 2? This step tells us there is a Power greater than ourselves that can restore us to sanity—and here we may need this Power. Resentment may be making us insane.

There was a particularly wise woman who was in both AA and Al-Anon. She did not have an easy life, but she was making it—one day at a time. She once said: "In the morning I pray for three things: "that God will help me not pick up a drink, that He will take away the awful, burning resentment I feel, and that He will help me have a good day."

The majority of us probably don't have to worry about not picking up the drink. Do you know how lucky this makes us? But dollars to donuts, the majority of us do carry a lot of resentment. Why wouldn't we? Experiencing the embarrassment of foolish, stupid behavior, the lack of responsibility on the part of the alcoholic, and sometimes various kinds of abuse are enough to put anybody on the Pity Pot. And that's only a tiny step from bitterly resenting the alcoholic, our burdens, our families, our lives. And we should acknowledge that this resentment hurts us far more than it hurts the addicted person.

So we ask for help. Help from our Higher Power, help from our 12-Step group, help from a counselor or therapist, if we have one. Then we can make the effort to change our thoughts—no easy task, but a necessary and useful one. No two bodies can occupy the same space at the same time, nor can two thoughts. When we feel resentment creeping in, we could change the thought. We may have to do this dozens/hundreds/thousands of times, but it does work. We could substitute a happy or humorous or grateful thought.

> I find the best antidote for resentment is the
> continual practice of gratitude.
> Al-Anon Member

Would you believe the practice of gratitude may do as much to benefit us as the practice of resentment did to harm us? We can also stop holding on to thoughts that make us feel used, abused, or inadequate. With effort we can let them go:

> "The horror of that moment," the King went on,
> "I shall never, NEVER forget!"
> "You will, though," the Queen said,
> "if you don't make a memorandum of it."
> Lewis Carroll[57]

---

[57] Lewis Carroll, *Through the Looking Glass* (Boston: Lothrop Publishing Co., 1898), 115.

Can we see that resentment is a destructive way (mainly to us) of thinking and feeling and that it is in our best interest to let go of it? In this letting go, we may need help—from our Higher Power and perhaps also from our 12-Step group, sponsor, or therapist.

We can also practice the habit of watching our thoughts and substituting positive, grateful ones for negative ones. Dealing with resentment and working to eradicate it from our thoughts and life will do more than almost anything to bring us a measure of joy—regardless of what else is going on.

◁☺▷

OPTIONS

It is reported that Brigham Young, a prophet of the Church of Jesus Christ of Latter-day Saints, once said that if you get bit by a rattlesnake, you can 1) Chase down the snake and beat it to death, or 2) Get rid of the venom as quickly as possible. If you choose the second option, he said, you will probably survive; if you choose the first, you won't have time for anything else.[58]

---

[58] See Marion D. Hanks, "Forgiveness: The Ultimate Form of Love," *Ensign*, Jan. 1974, 20.

The Power of Gratitude

Wallowing in resentment or self-pity is dangerous.
Wallowing in gratitude is sublime.
Anonymous

∽

Think of resentment as a deadly poison that we have too much of in our mind and body. Is there an antidote? There is, and we can access it at any time. The antidote is (...drum roll...) GRATITUDE.

Well, some of us don't feel a bit like being grateful. No one understands. We're living with an awful, stressful thing. (Did someone call it a disease?) How can we be grateful for something as horrible as alcoholism or addiction? And why should we be?

The answer might be another question: do we want to feel better? If we really do, then we might be desperate enough to try anything, even something that at first seems foolish. It is possible to switch from resentment and anger to gratitude by reviewing things we can be grateful for right now.

To begin, we might make a gratitude list. Can we find something to be thankful for? If we really work at it, maybe we can. Lots of people find it useful to make lists—for shopping, activities, and commitments—so why not for gratitude? In this case, we could list the things that are pretty good today. Like what? The sun came up this morning—it may be raining, but above the rain clouds, we know the sun is there. Chances are we had something to eat for breakfast. Most likely we have a roof over our heads. And probably cars or buses to get us places. Maybe jobs to go to. There are probably a few people who care about us. They may be annoying, but it's sort of nice to not be alone. But aloneness isn't bad either. It may be the opportunity we need to check out where we are and where we might like to be and how to get there. Sometimes kids are instructed to list something to be thankful for beginning with each letter of the alphabet, from aardvarks and apples to zebras and zucchini—for those who don't like zucchini, there's always Zingers. Then, when we feel down and dirty, we can read our list and perhaps get a chuckle and some food for thought (like Zingers).

Some find that it helps to look at their defects of character through the lens of gratitude. They may see that these defects were useful in protecting them in the past, so they deserve gratitude. After a quick "thanks" to the formerly useful defects, they can say "bye bye" and gratefully move on. (This doesn't happen immediately.)

Looking at others, especially at 12-Step meetings where more than the superficial is shared, we often become grateful that our problems are not as bad as someone else's. And if we could see ALL that's going on in someone's life, we'd likely opt for our own problems—and even be grateful for them.

One thing we can learn to be grateful for is that we only have to tackle our own burdens each day and we don't have to take on someone else's burdens or burdens that will be ours next month or next year.

It's useful to start our day with prayers of gratitude, especially for the presence of our Higher Power, who provides light and wisdom for whatever comes during the day. It might also be useful to give as much time to thoughts of gratitude as we give to thoughts of our woes. Better still, give double time to gratitude. Best of all, chuck the whining and self-pity and resentment and zero in on gratitude and gratitude only! (Easier said than done.) There's nothing like gratitude to lift up our negative thoughts into a positive realm of beauty and even health.

> I used to say, "Life sucks and things can't get any worse," and somehow they always did. Now I take each day as a gift and am grateful for it and my life just keeps getting better.
> Tim, AA member

It's a good idea to not become complacent, but to try to think, feel, and speak gratitude for all the good in life, especially for what we've been taking for granted. And why waste life fretting over the small stuff when we can expand our world by the practice of gratitude?

Each day is a new adventure to be lived in humility and gratitude. Practice seeing everything with a fresh eye, detached from resentment—if only temporarily. Then turn away from negative thoughts and focus only on the positive things for which you are grateful. Every experience can be a gift if seen in the light of gratitude.

Difficult situations and even character defects can provide us with opportunities for growth that we would not have had otherwise. Remember the story of Dorothy and her companions in *The Wizard of Oz*? The Cowardly Lion learned he already had courage, the Brainless Scarecrow learned he already had intelligence, and the Heartless Tin Man learned he did, indeed, have a heart. The difficult experiences they had together brought out each one's unique potential. Even Dorothy got back to Kansas. Some might question whether the black and white Kansas of the movie was really superior to the colorful and exciting Land of Oz, but "there's no place like home."

Someone has suggested that we be grateful for problems themselves because if they have brought us to prayer, they have served a good purpose. How many of us would choose the work it takes to grow into a relationship with a Higher Power? But in the aftermath of this hard work, brought on by our problems, we often gain a serenity and competence for which we can be most grateful.

We can be grateful for any answers to our prayers, even ones we don't want. A problem could be a form of assistance, or it could hold a hidden blessing. Looking back and seeing our progress can be an occasion for gratitude, no matter what is happening in our lives. Gratitude can be a tool we use to shape our lives for the better. Resentment will lessen as we keep a gratitude list or take a little time every day to be thankful.

> They told me to say "Thanks" for everything. I didn't feel like it but I did. I went out and said, "Thanks for the sunset. Thanks for the birds." Big Deal! But, as I continued to do this, I realized it WAS a Big Deal. As I said "Thanks" on a daily, even hourly basis, I began to feel truly grateful and, oddly, my life got better. I now see the glass as half full instead of half empty, and that has made all the difference.
> Joyce, AA/Al-Anon member

Awareness of the good in life increases with the practice of gratitude. We always have a choice—a choice of response, if nothing else. To respond with gratitude, while sometimes difficult, can be rewarding and can lead to a higher, more peaceful life, a life filled with serenity and joy.

Sometimes people attending an AA meeting for the first time are amazed to hear someone say, "I thank God I'm an alcoholic."

Even more mind blowing is hearing a spouse say, "I thank God I married an alcoholic." What are these people? Crazy? Chances are no one is grateful for the disease of alcoholism, but people can be grateful for the blessings brought by recovery and learning better ways to live.

About another disease:

> My cancer was the best thing that ever happened to me.
> Lance Armstrong

And here's what one of the co-founders of Al-Anon had to say:

> I never felt alcoholism did something "to me,"
> it did something "for me!"
> Anne B.

If anyone had reason to whine and be ungrateful, it would be Helen Keller, who was blind and deaf. Helen has been quoted as saying, "I am grateful for my handicap. Through it, I have found my work, my God, and myself." This doesn't sound much like whining, does it?

Can we be grateful for the possibility of progressing from Victim to Survivor? And then change from Survivor to Winner?

How important is gratitude? Think about these words that have survived since the dawn of the fourteenth century:

> If the only prayer you said in your whole life was,
> "Thank You," that would suffice.
> Meister Eckhart[59]

---

[59] Al-Anon, *Courage to Change* (Al-Anon Family Group Headquarters, 1992), 340. Eckhart von Hochheim was a German mystic who lived from 1260 to 1327.

◁☺▷
WHERE DO THEY COME UP WITH THESE??

Dear God,

Why is Sunday School always on Sunday? I thought it was supposed to be a day of rest.

Tom

Dear God,

Thank You for the baby brother. But what I prayed for was a puppy.

Joyce

Dear God,

Do You really mean, "Do unto others as they do unto you?" Because if You do, I'm going to hit my brother.

Dana

Dear God,

Did You mean for the giraffe to look like that, or was it an accident?

Norma

Dear God,

In school they told us what You do. Who does it when You are on vacation?

Jane

How to Forgive

The bottom line is, blame doesn't work. What does work?
Love and forgiveness.
Unknown

To forgive is to set the prisoner free and then
discover the prisoner was you.
Unknown

As we have mentioned, resentment and its bedfellows, self-pity and anger, conspire to keep us from being all we can be. Being in a state of blame or having uncharitable thoughts, especially of revenge, saps our energy, blinds us, and leaves us open to a variety of bad stuff, including physical and mental illness. Gratitude can help, but it is not enough.

FORGIVENESS is the other antidote for the anger and blame that resentment brings.

Who wants to stay in a state of *agita*? What, you ask, is agita (AH-je-ta)? From *Merriam-Webster*: "South Italian dialect pronunciation of Italian acido, literally, heartburn, acid, from Latin acidus...a feeling of agitation or anxiety." Loosely defined, agita is a word that means a churning of the emotions, often becoming a churning of the guts—absolutely not a good feeling. Most of us experience agita at one time or another. The purposeful practice of forgiveness can help the agita dissipate.

Can we see an annoying or hurtful situation in any other way? A modern self-help author, Dr. Wayne W. Dyer, says, "Change the way you look at things, and the things you look at will change."[60] (Is the glass half full or half empty??)

---

[60] Wayne W. Dyer, *The Power of Intention* (New York: Hay House, Inc., 2004).

Is this possible? Maybe. Not many of us have really tried it. Our inner dialogue, which keeps mulling over a bad situation, keeps the resentful event or feeling on the front burner, so to speak, and may contribute to its perpetuation. People in recovery often say, "When I am in my head, I am behind enemy lines." Or, "My negative thoughts are unwanted tenants who have taken up residence in my head and aren't paying rent."

Our own negativity is bad enough, yet many of us take on the negativity of other people, too. We might ask ourselves if we would be better off avoiding mental agreement with the negative opinions of others.

Is it in our own best interest to hang on to nasty, vengeful thoughts? Do they help our disposition, creativity, mental, or physical health?

One of the U.S.'s early female physicians was a Dr. Cady, who practiced in New York City around the turn of the 20th century. She was years, even decades, ahead of her time, a pioneer in psychosomatic medicine and spiritual healing. She was pretty forthright in her diagnosis of resentment and its contribution to illness, along with its antidote of forgiveness. She said, "...[W]e must also forgive as we would be forgiven....you may think 'I've got no one to forgive!' Yet if we consider all the people we feel negativity toward, or that we think 'served him right,' then we find we have much to forgive. Any pain that you suffer, any failure of some expected good, may be the result of a spirit of unforgiveness you're holding toward someone in particular or the world in general."[61]

Forgiveness does not mean that we have to accept unacceptable behavior. Forgiving may involve letting go of a relationship. If we forgive before moving on, we are not bound to the past. In this sense, forgiveness can be cutting the threads binding us to a relationship along with its negativity. On the other hand, forgiving someone may involve informing that person of our discomfort or anger related to their behavior, which could lead to a mutually beneficial exchange of thoughts and feelings.

We might ask, "Am I willing to give someone power over me?" Isn't that what we do when we fail to forgive?

It is said there is freedom and power in forgiveness. Our own experiences may have shown us that holding resentments and grudges keeps us trapped in a snare of negativity. To keep thinking of them is like holding our own heads under a sea of rotting, slimy

---

[61] H. Emilie Cady, *Lessons in Truth* (1896).

sewage. Turning from these resentments and grudges through forgiveness can let us breathe more easily and allows us to focus on good things and God's plan for our lives. (Also allows for shampoo and a shower.)

Yes, it is easy to see the freedom that can come with forgiveness. But power? Does forgiving other people give us power over them? No, no, and NO! Forgiveness gives us power over our own thoughts and feelings. The Bible tells us that it is better to rule our thoughts (spirit) than to take a city (Prov. 16:32). We have power over our own thoughts only. Forgiveness does not give us power to control others. We can say nearly all human beings have offended and hurt one another—intentionally or unintentionally. Forgiving takes away the blame and resentment that are so harmful to US and replaces them with joy and peace. Our serenity may depend on our willingness and ability to forgive.

Forgiveness might be easier if we can remember that those who offended us were likely doing the best they knew how at the time of the offense. So were we. If we could see how our own behavior is often less than desirable, we might be better able to forgive our offenders and ourselves.

The Bible says, "Judge not, and ye shall not be judged; condemn not, and ye shall not be condemned: forgive and ye shall be forgiven" (Luke 6:37). Could this mean that I get what I give out? Does it mean that the great justice of the universe will treat me as I am treating others, will give good or ill to me as I am giving to others, and will forgive me my imperfections in the same way I am forgiving others theirs? Am I forgiving the rotten S.O.B.s because it is in MY best interest to do so? (And if they are still, to me, rotten S.O.B.s, maybe I have not quite done the necessary forgiving.) Do I need to forgive myself—and be forgiven by my Higher Power—for judging others? These questions could provoke a lot of thought.

There are degrees of offenses and thus degrees of difficulty in forgiving. Someone stepping on your foot is one thing, someone stealing your car is another, and someone betraying your trust is yet another. Make sure you don't put someone stepping on your foot in the same category as someone who betrays your trust.

Forgiveness can be a process. It may not happen all at once and may need to be repeated—sort of like getting rid of crabgrass. Or ants. But what a relief to finally realize the crabgrass is gone and there are no more ants crawling over the sink. Even better is the relief we feel when we realize our ugly, resentful thoughts are a thing of the past.

There are some things that are particularly difficult to forgive. One young woman, after great effort, just could not forgive her father for his horrible abuse of her mother. A woman she looked up to told her to stop trying, to give it to God, and let Him make her ready to forgive in His own time. In other words, let go and let God. (We hear that a lot in recovery programs.)

We've all heard people say: "I can forgive but I can't forget." Can they? Hanging on to old thoughts of hurt while trying to move on is like wearing leg irons while trying to move toward a destination. Even if the destination is reached, we have spent way too much time getting there. (This does not mean that you should not learn a lesson from past experiences—i.e., fool me once, shame on you; fool me twice, shame on me).

There is the possibility that a nasty situation or hateful person in our life might be a message from our Higher Power that we need to take some kind of action or learn some kind of lesson. If nothing else, it might be nudging us to work on our conscious contact with our Higher Power (Step 11). Remember, "if my problems have brought me to prayer, they have served a purpose."

Forgiveness can involve a change of attitude. As Dr. Dyer—quoted earlier—said, "Change the way you look at things and the things you look at will change."

Forgiving within the family can be particularly challenging. These are the people nearest and dearest to us; thus they know which of our buttons to push and are aware of how to be most hurtful. They may be the hardest to forgive—also the most important to forgive. Can we give our parents/children and ourselves the gift of forgiveness?

An Al-Anon mom says, "One day I did something particularly hurtful to my sons. I felt bad and asked, 'Can you boys forgive me?' Their friend from two houses up was there and put it in perspective, saying, 'Now, Mrs. Armstrong, do you forgive Grandma Rogers for the things she did to you when you were a kid?' 'Oh yeah, I guess so.' And with his 10-year-old wisdom, David said, 'Well, then, John and Mike forgive you.'"

We do ourselves—and others—a favor by making the effort to stay in a state of forgiveness.

The best way to get even is to forget.

Too many people offer God prayers with
claw marks all over them.

◁ ☺ ▷

"Do you really believe that someone can actually tell
the future by looking at cards?"
"Yes, I do. My mother takes one look at my report card and then tells me exactly
what's going to happen to me when my father comes home."

Spirituality and Religion

*God is a Spirit and they that worship him must
worship him in spirit and in truth.*
John 4:24

~

Aren't spirituality and religion the same?

They are often considered together and sometimes the words are used interchangeably. If they are not the same, then how do they differ? And who cares?

The 12-Step Program of recovery is one of spirituality, although it has no religious connection. People involved in any 12-Step program are encouraged to come to a belief in a power greater than themselves.

So how are spirituality and religion different? First, let's look at religion. According to the dictionary, each religion has its own set of beliefs. One will find doctrine, celebration of holy days, scripture, etc., and each is practiced in temples, churches, mosques, synagogues, or other places of worship. Religion has been studied, debated, philosophized upon, argued over, and even fought over. Crusades and Twin Towers, inquisitions and wars—all these have been the results of religious beliefs. Religions also contribute significantly to art, education, and charitable works.

One dictionary defines spirituality as the act of being spiritual. Now, that is a real help. We might say spirituality is the relationship between an individual and his or her Higher Power. While it is possible for one to be both spiritual and religious (that is one definition among several in one dictionary) at the same time, there is no requirement to have one in order to have the other.

Have you noticed that deeply spiritual people are humble people? So it would seem that humility is one of the attributes of spirituality. In a program of recovery from addiction—or co-dependency—the person who "gets the program" wants to throw away pretenses, to become humble in the sense of teachable, mold-able. Ideally such a person does not look down on anyone, nor is he or she awed by those possessing the beauty, material goods, or prominent positions people usually revered—and sometimes reviled—by the media.

In treating an alcoholic/addict, the one who has hit bottom and feels the despondency of the situation seems to be the one easiest to treat. Such people have lost all pride and self-delusion and have become humble by circumstances. Someone who has everything and is "doing OK" is the hardest to work with. After all, how can we answer a person who says, "There can't be anything wrong with me—just look at my job/family/whatever." The concept of making someone "hit bottom" is part of the intervention process used to get some people into treatment. Remember Betty Ford?[62]

Let's mention the first three of the 12 Steps again:

- We admitted we were powerless over alcohol (or drugs, or...), that our lives had become unmanageable.
- Came to believe that a Power greater than ourselves could restore us to sanity.
- Made a decision to turn our will and our lives over to the care of God, as we understood Him.

One of the hardest things we have to do is admit that we are powerless, that we are not in control. Most of us feel we can (and even must) control our lives and the lives of those nearest and dearest to us. If we will just work harder, if we will just live in the right place, if we will send our children to the right schools, etc., etc., everything will work out the way we want it to. September 11th demonstrated that the world can change in an instant, but many of us still cling to the illusion that we can, by force of will, make things the way we want them.

When someone close to us is addicted, it's easy to see a life out of control and, knowing what is best for our loved one, we tend to

---

[62] Betty Ford (b. 1918), First Lady to President Gerald Ford, breast cancer survivor, and equal rights advocate. The Ford family ran an intervention in 1978, forcing Betty to confront alcoholism and addiction to opioid analgesics. She went on to establish a treatment center and worked to help recovering individuals.

become obsessed with fixing the situation. We become out of control trying to control the addicted person. HOLD IT!

Step 1 tells that us we are powerless. This is the last thing we want to hear. But many will tell us that this step is the most important step. We need to recognize and acknowledge our powerlessness over alcohol and the disease of alcoholism, which is often called a cunning, powerful, and baffling disease. Our lives have truly become unmanageable. This is the bad news.

The good news comes with Step 2. The good news is that there is a Power greater than ourselves and this Power can restore us to sanity.

Step 3 lets us in on the secret. It is to surrender to this Power that is greater than we are, the turning of will and life over to the care of this greater Power, to which many give the name God. Not everyone is comfortable with the word God; some prefer the term Higher Power. In any case, we give up our puny efforts to control the uncontrollable and turn it all over to this Power greater than ourselves. We let go.

Let go of what? Let go of trying to run the world, to control everyone and everything. That is a good start. And where do spirituality and religion come in? Well, we don't need religion to do this. But we do need to call on something to take over what we cannot control. This Higher Power is available to us through a spiritual awareness. The awareness sometimes comes like an explosion, but this is rare. Awareness usually comes in small increments and as a gradual overall growth. It happens when we come to believe in the Higher Power as the real one in control, not ourselves. We do not have to be grounded in any religious philosophy to recognize a Power greater than ourselves. The thunderstorm that just passed had far more power than we do. We do not make the flowers bloom, nor do we make the sun rise and set. We do not make a baby breathe and move and cry. A Power far greater than ourselves does all these things. Do these not bring a sense of awe when we behold them? And recognizing this can be a very spiritual occurrence, and it can happen without any particular reference to any religion.

We say that AA, Al-Anon, Alateen, and all other 12-Step programs are spiritual, not religious. They endorse no religion and leave such matters to their individual members. It may be mentioned that most people, after being in a 12-Step program for some period of time, return to the religion they were brought up in. This is a matter of their own independent decision, without pushing, cajoling, or help from the group.

Spirituality is one of those things that for most people takes time. It does develop when one follows the right steps. And we might note that humility develops when we realize just how powerless we have become in controlling another person.

As we have mentioned already, the famous psychoanalyst Carl Jung sent alcoholics away, telling them he couldn't help them with their illness; the only alcoholics he knew who got well had experienced a spiritual event, which had nothing to do with him. Spiritual experiences help us gain confidence to overcome the challenges associated with alcoholism.

Here is a story of the explosive kind of spiritual event:

I was sitting in an AA meeting, not paying much attention to what was being said, because my mind was elsewhere. I was having that nightmare of the alcoholic of "never having another drink." I found myself lost. I felt completely powerless! I knew not where to turn. All the negative feelings were upon me and I didn't know what to do, or how I would do it. In my mind, I kept thinking, "How can I do this?" I felt so completely lost and adrift; I was overwhelmed by the feelings.

Then a voice, just as clear as a bell, said to me that it would be all right. The voice came from near the door at the front right of the meeting room. It continued to reassure me all would be well, I would be able to not drink again, and it showed me many future events. Many have already come true, including that I would not drink again. That was twenty years ago. I then knew that I had a "Higher Power" and this Power would help me through the tough times. As with most alcoholics, I was spiritually bankrupt until that moment that touched me and turned my life around.

Len, AA member

This experience is rare. Far more common is the conversion that takes place in small steps. The seeds of spirituality are sown in little increments that often go unnoticed when they first occur. They are planted in small quantities by letting go of some control here, leaning on the Higher Power there, and recognizing some powerlessness over yonder. The seeds grow slowly and are often not noticed until it is almost time for the harvest. There are dry spells and cold days to set them back, but the growth process resumes and blossoms form. And to use the old cliché, from tiny acorns, great oaks grow.

Spirituality is more of a feeling, more like love, than like any intellectual pursuit. It is not like religion in that it has no theology or dogma attached. When spirituality takes over our lives, there is a newfound peace with ourselves and our situations. There is a new ability to face adversity with calmness and strength. It allows us to see things for what they really are, not what our mind wants to make of them. It is a form of personal magic in dealing with life's challenges.

To show that religion and spirituality do not necessarily go together, here are examples of people we are familiar with: Abraham Lincoln is considered to be the most devout, "religious" president of the United States, although he had no formal religion. He was a spiritual person. On the other hand, those who blew up the World Trade Center were religious to the point of giving their lives for their religion. But would we call them spiritual?

◁☺▷
QUIZ

Q. How many psychiatrists does it take to change a light bulb?
A. One, but the light bulb has to want to change.

Q. How many doctors does it take to screw in a light bulb?
A. Three: one to find a bulb specialist, one to find a bulb installation specialist, and one to bill it all to Medicare.

Q. How many policemen does it take to screw in a light bulb?
A. None, it turns itself in.

Q. How many nuclear engineers does it take to change a light bulb?
A. Seven, one to install the new bulb and six to figure out what to do with the old one for the next 10,000 years.

Q. How many Bill Gateses does it take to change a light bulb?
A. One, he puts in the bulb and lets the world revolve around him.

Q. How many Californians does it take to change a light bulb?
A. Five, one to turn the bulb and four to relate to the experience.

Q. How many Floridians does it take to change a light bulb?
A. We don't know. They're still counting.

Q. How many babysitters does it take to change a light bulb?
A. None. They don't make Pampers that small.

Q. How many men does it take to put up a toilet seat?
A. We don't know. It's never happened.

Meditation

In the midst of movement and chaos, keep stillness inside of you.
Deepak Chopra[63]

∼

Does our idea of meditation include an old guy with a long white beard and robe sitting on a mountaintop in Tibet? It could also be a young guy in a suit taking deep breaths to calm himself as he sits in a traffic jam in Toronto. Or a young mother in Tallahassee with children fussing and clamoring for her attention sitting in her bathroom taking a few minutes to center her emotions so she won't kill them all. Or a middle-aged executive in Texas who shuts the office door and quiets outside thoughts to wait in silence for an answer.

All these could be pictures of meditation.

We might say that prayer is talking to God and that meditation is listening. In our culture, we'd rather talk. Step 11 tells us we need both talking and listening. The daily practice of meditation is recommended for our health. It can also put us in touch with and bring us closer to our Higher Power.

A wise person has said that there are good as well as bad addictions. One could replace addiction to a substance/behavior/person with an addiction to meditation, to seeking and finding God on a daily basis.

A Jesuit priest who had interest in Eastern religions said he could take a passage of scripture and meditate on it. Or he could also empty himself, asking God to fill him if He chose to do so. "And sometimes He does."

---

[63] Deepak Chopra (b. 1946), American physician, speaker, writer on spirituality and mind-body medicine.

PRACTICAL MEDITATION

When we say Practical Meditation, does this mean the meditation used with prayer is impractical? Nothing could be further from the truth. But meditation can be expanded.

No one needs to tell us we live in a stressful age. And dealing with addiction raises our stress level. Most of us have had experiences of stress causing physical problems.

According to the Harvard Medical School Special Heath Report on Stress Management:

> You may define stress as bumper-to-bumper traffic...the need to care for an ailing parent or a pile of unpaid bills.

> Stress itself can be defined more broadly as an automatic physical response to any stimulus that requires you to adjust to change.

> Muscles tense. Breathing quickens, and beads of sweat appear. But actually, how and why these reactions occur and what effects they might have over time are questions that have intrigued researchers for many years.

At Harvard Medical School the study of stress has been going on for decades. The shell-shocked soldiers of World War I caught the attention of Walter B. Cannon,[64] a Harvard physiologist who began to explore the biochemistry of fright. His research convinced him that fright was not all in the mind, but also stemmed from the adrenal glands, which sit atop the kidneys. During experiments with barking dogs and caged cats, Cannon was able to isolate a hormone secreted by the adrenal glands of the frightened cats.

When he injected that hormone into a second perfectly calm cat, it touched off a physical reaction of fear. The cat's heartbeat and blood pressure shot up, while blood flow to the muscles increased. Cannon dubbed this occurrence the "fright, fight, or flight response." Currently, though, it's known as "fight or flight" or the "stress response."

So that's how it is. Most of us have experienced the tense muscles, quick breathing, and pulsing blood pressure. We've got the stress response. So what can we do about it? Ever hear of the relaxation response? What?

Let's go back to Harvard Medical School where Cannon did his cat-unfriendly experiments on stress. In the early 1970s, Dr. Herbert

---

[64]Walter B. Cannon (1871–1945), American physiologist, coined term "flight or fight response."

Benson,[65] a cardiologist, began researching the damaging effects of stress and the body's potential for self-healing. He found that the effects of stress could be minimized by what he called the relaxation response. He said, "The relaxation response is the opposite of the stress response. It is a state of profound rest and release. By regularly practicing techniques that evoke the relaxation response, you can help your body erase the cumulative effects of stress." Dr. Benson found that regular meditation would lower oxygen consumption, slow heartbeat and respiration, and decrease blood pressure. What a wonderful fringe benefit for seeking to improve our conscious contact with God through prayer and meditation!

◁☺▷

NOAH'S ARK

You can learn everything you need to know about life from Noah's Ark.
1. Don't miss the boat.
2. Remember that we are all in the same boat.
3. Plan ahead. It wasn't raining when Noah built the Ark.
4. Stay fit. When you're 800 years old, someone may ask you to do something really big.
5. Don't listen to critics. Just get on with the job that needs to be done.
6. Build your future on high ground.
7. For safety's sake, travel in pairs.
8. Speed isn't always an advantage. The snails were on board with the cheetahs.
9. When you're stressed, float for a while.
10. Remember, the ark was built by amateurs, and the *Titanic* was built by professionals.

---

[65] Herbert Benson, MD (b. 1935), American cardiologist, pioneer in mind-body research.

The Serenity Prayer

Up in the mornin', out on the job
Work like the devil for my pay
But that lucky old sun has nothin' to do
But roll around heaven all day.
"That Lucky Old Sun"

Haven Gillespie[66] had a great idea when he wrote those lyrics. It sounds like the sun has an ideal life with no troubles at all. We've known people who seem to have idyllic lives, with no trouble or heartache, but when we get to know them better, we find there is a masquerade party going on and seldom, if ever, is there the peace and serenity that we are led to believe exists in this perfect life. Perhaps instead of rolling around heaven, we might better be singing "Raindrops Keep Falling on My Head." As we've discovered, if something can go wrong, it probably will. And worst of all, we can't control it. Try to stop the raindrops. But it would seem that we really need them to keep the world from drying up and blowing away like sands in the desert. And like plants in the soil, we need some rain to enable us to grow. If it were not for sorrow and sadness, how would we ever appreciate happiness and joy? If not for pain and sickness, how would we recognize health and physical well-being? And if not for the sorrow of separation, how would we know love and friendship? Around and around goes the circle of life to bring us the full bag of emotions and feelings.

We don't want tough experiences and can sometimes be incapacitated by them if we don't know how to handle them, or are, for

---

[66] Haven Gillespie (1888–1975). His most famous song is "Santa Claus Is Coming to Town."

whatever reason, unable to process and deal with them. So what can we do to help ourselves through the trials and vicissitudes of life? Is there a Magic Bullet that will, if not insulate us from trouble, enable us to handle it? We may be lucky if we suffer disappointments and setbacks as children if they nudge us into some growth and prepare us for the bigger disappointments and setbacks that come to us as adults. Being chosen last for a playground game may get us ready for when we aren't chosen for the promotion we want. Handling the death of a beloved pet can pave the way for handling the eventual death of a parent.

There are people who have been so kicked about by life that they form a shell around themselves that can't be penetrated by the emotions of either joy or sorrow. They are spared the trauma of tragedy but also the euphoria of triumph. Most of us would not choose or be capable of succumbing to this kind of catatonic numbness; rather, we'd prefer, as TV's "Wide World of Sports" described it, "the thrill of victory and the agony of defeat."

There are a few words, actually twenty-six of them, that can help us in these situations where we are powerless. Ever hear of the Serenity Prayer?

God grant me the Serenity
To accept the things I cannot change,
Courage to change the things I can,
And the Wisdom to know the difference.

Where did this prayer come from? There are those who tell us the ideas go back centuries, to St. Francis of Assisi, to the ancient Greeks and Romans, maybe even to the Sanskrit.

Reinhold Niebuhr (1892–1971) was head of the Union Theological Seminary in New York City for many years. His most famous work is *Moral Man in Immoral Society: A Study of Ethics and Politics*. Few of us are familiar with that or his other works—and few of us care. But the little prayer he penned has touched millions.

In its original form it was much longer and went like this:

God, give us grace to accept with serenity
The things that cannot be changed.
Courage to change the things
Which should be changed;
And the Wisdom to distinguish
The one from the other.
Living one day at a time,
Enjoying one moment at a time,

144

Accepting hardships as the pathway to peace.
Taking, as He did, this sinful world
As it is, not as I would have it;
Trusting that He will make all things right
If I surrender to His Will;
That I may be reasonably happy in this life
And supremely happy with Him
Forever in the next.
AMEN![67]

Members of AA, Al-Anon, or other 12-Step groups may tell you they know people for whom the Serenity Prayer made the difference between sanity and insanity and some few for whom it meant the difference between life and death. It is that powerful!

It seems quite simple when we take it line by line. First, we ask the God of our understanding, the Higher Power, however we personally define that, to grant us (give us as a free gift) the serenity we need. And that serenity is the ability to accept the thing that has happened that is the source of pain to us. And since this is something that has happened already, we cannot just make it go away! Well, what if it is something we can do something about? Then we pray for the courage to do what is necessary to make the changes we can make. We are not asking to change things we have no means of changing. What we also need now is the knowledge (wisdom) to know if there is something we can and should change. Now you have far more than twenty-six words trying to say what the prayer says in its simplicity and wisdom. Here is a story of the Serenity Prayer making a difference:

> "The worst-case scenario has come to pass," my husband said as he picked me up from work. I knew that meant our son had crossed the line from HIV to full-blown AIDS.
>
> This was a time when little was known about the disease, just that it was horrible, devastating, and most likely fatal.
>
> We parents, who had tried (despite our imperfections and screw-ups) to protect our kids and keep them safe and healthy, were totally powerless to change the dreaded diagnosis. I felt shaky and full of stress. I began to pray silently. Almost immediately, the inner voice told me to repeat the Serenity Prayer. I did over and over and over. My husband was doing the same thing.

---

[67] Reinhold Neibuhr, *The Essential Reinhold Niebuhr: Selected Essays and Addresses.* Edited by Robert McAfee Brown (New Haven: Yale University Press, 1987), 25.

Eventually we felt a sense of calm. He related that he had seen a rainbow over the highway. I looked and saw the end of it, only a fragment, but it was a rainbow, a symbol of hope. There was no way to change anything; we could only offer love and support to our son. Acceptance of the unacceptable was the only sensible course of action.

> If you accept, things are the way they are.
> If you do not accept, things are the way they are.
> Zen proverb

A member of one group has said:

> God grant me the Serenity to accept the
> people I cannot change,
> Courage to change the person I can,
> And Wisdom to know it's me!

We've mentioned that in the program, we are encouraged to develop a sense of humor. Some jokers have made humorous versions of the Serenity Prayer. Here is one:

> God, grant me the serenity to accept what I can't
> change, courage to change what I can, and wisdom
> to hide the bodies of those who p***d me off.

◁ ☺ ▷

If the grass is greener on the other side of the fence, you can
bet the water bill is also higher!
Anonymous

Two Prayers

Pray without ceasing.
I Thessalonians 5:17

~

Here are two examples of prayer that are dramatic and unusual: the Prayer of Total Desperation and the Prayer of Total Trust.

First, the Prayer of Total Desperation:

Linda was an alcoholic. She had been going to AA for three months and felt worse than ever. She couldn't imagine herself never having another drink. She went to meetings and did what they suggested but was "white knuckling" it all the way.

One evening Linda couldn't stand it anymore. She had to have a drink. She got in her car and drove to a nearby bar. She sat in the car for a few minutes, contemplating what she was doing. If she took the drink, there would be three months of hard work and anguish down the drain. But she just had to have that drink.

Linda remembered what she'd heard in the meetings about God and prayer and didn't think it had anything to do with her. But in a last desperate attempt to avoid the drink, she said: "Listen here, God, I don't even think You exist. But if You do, then dammit, don't let me go in there!"

A sweet, peaceful feeling came over her. She put the key back in the ignition and drove home and had no more desire to drink. She called it the beginning of her recovery, and at the time she told this story, she'd had fourteen years of sobriety.

The experience was the beginning of Linda's recovery, but it was only the beginning. She continued with AA, worked through the 12 Steps, and devoted much time to helping other alcoholics.

Now, the Prayer of Total Trust:

L. Emma "Becky" Brodbeck was a nonagenarian a couple of us had the privilege of meeting. She was one of the youngest adults we knew. She spent her ninetieth birthday going a thousand miles up the Amazon River in a dugout canoe, even though she had trouble seeing, hearing, and walking. She had a serenity to be envied, and we often think of her as the "let go/let God lady." Her serenity came in large part from an experience she'd had some years earlier.

Becky Brodbeck was the opposite of Linda. From childhood, she'd had great faith and a great desire to serve God, so she went to China as a missionary around 1915. She was in the city of Losan in Szechuan Province—famed for its hot food—at the time of World War II.

After the war, with the Communists taking over, many missionaries left the country. Becky, who had no dependents, chose to stay, hoping to help ease the transition for the people she had come to love. It didn't work that way.

The Communists had plans that didn't include God or His servants. Becky was under house arrest for many months and was taken to jail twice. Here is her story of her second arrest and incarceration from her book, *China Farewell*:

> One of the police we especially disliked seemed to hover in the background most of the day, egging on my tormentors. His duties were probably assigned, but it seemed that he executed them with fervor and joy. He had recently made serious trouble for neighbors, reporting them for a slight indiscretion, so that both father and eldest son had been in prison for the last month. He came frequently in the house and annoyed us endlessly. Early in our association with him the Canadians and I had nicknamed him "Pet Police."

> Pet Police led me across the compound, calling to underlings to bring the key. Again the door of my little jail room swung inward, then banged shut.

> The room was empty. After the glare of sunshine, it seemed wholly dark and pleasantly cool. There was the old familiar bed—dirty straw covering the bare boards. I smelled the mustiness of the closed up room. I fingered the dirty straw. It had been winter when I lived there before but now summer was coming and the insects were already lively. "Fleas, if nothing worse" I thought. "I'll just stand here, not trusting myself to that dirty straw."

148

Then I realized how nervously tired I was. It had been a long, hard day, nor would this be the end of it. The real trouble was only beginning. If I were to be in jail, I'd get acquainted with fleas and bedbugs and lice and mosquitoes. What difference would that make if that acquaintance began a few hours earlier? I lay down and relaxed. It was dark and cool, and I was exhausted. I slept.

It was only a short sleep until the door was flung open. A shaft of late afternoon sunlight shone directly into my eyes and I was suddenly wide-awake. There was Pet Police leaning over me and looking down into my eyes as I opened them. I saw his frightened expression.

"You're praying again," he muttered. Then with his usual authoritative voice repeated, "You're praying again. How many times have I told you prayer is an old superstition?"

But I had caught his look and the note of fear in his voice. He had always seemed curious about our Christian custom of prayer and had asked many questions. In writing my life history he had always wanted to add prayer to the list of my work duties. I had contended that prayer didn't belong there with scheduled activities such as teaching, visiting and holding regular meetings. I had told him over and over that prayer was a part of a Christian's life, an integral part, as necessary for the spirit as breathing and eating for the physical body. From the moment I saw his troubled look and heard the note of fear in his voice, I understood him better and hated him less. He tried not to believe in prayer but he feared its power. Poor boy! I suppose he couldn't imagine a prayer that was for any other purpose than calling down curses on the head of an enemy.

When he said, "You're praying again," I was suddenly ashamed. Here I was, in the worst predicament of my life. If ever prayer were indicated, surely this was the time. And I'd dropped off to sleep the moment I lay down. I now know that my falling asleep may have been the best prayer I've ever made, a prayer of trust. A frenzied prayer for help could never have calmed me and prepared me for the questioning to come, as did my short relaxing sleep. But at the moment I was ashamed. I evaded by saying, "I'm just resting. I've often told you that when I rest, I pray."

These two prayers, so different and by women in such different places, brought the desired results. Besides the immediate relief,

149

both developed a serenity that went far beyond the situations that called forth the prayers.

◁ ☺ ▷

CHILDREN ARE QUICK

TEACHER: Maria, go to the map and find North America.
MARIA: Here it is.

TEACHER: Correct. Now class, who discovered America?
CLASS: Maria.

TEACHER: John, why are you doing your math multiplication on the floor?
JOHN: You told me to do it without using tables.

TEACHER: Glen, how do you spell "crocodile?"
GLEN: K-R-O-K-O-D-I-A-L
TEACHER: No, that's wrong
GLEN: Maybe it is wrong, but you asked me how I spell it.
(I love this child.)

TEACHER: Donald, what is the chemical formula for water?
DONALD: H I J K L M N O.
TEACHER: What are you talking about?
DONALD: Yesterday you said it's H to O.

TEACHER: Winnie, name one important thing we have today that we didn't have ten years ago.
WINNIE: Me!

TEACHER: Glen, why do you always get so dirty?
GLEN: Well, I'm a lot closer to the ground than you are.

TEACHER: Millie, give me a sentence starting with "I."
MILLIE: I is...
TEACHER: No, Millie...Always say, "I am."
MILLIE: All right...I am the ninth letter of the alphabet.

TEACHER: George Washington not only chopped down his father's cherry tree but also admitted it. Now, Louis, do you know why his father didn't punish him?
LOUIS: Because George still had the axe in his hand?

TEACHER: Now, Simon, tell me frankly, do you say prayers before eating?
SIMON: No sir, I don't have to. My mom is a good cook.

TEACHER: Clyde, your composition on "My Dog" is exactly the same as your brother's...Did you copy his?
CLYDE: No, sir. It's the same dog.
(I want to adopt this kid!!!)

TEACHER: Harold, what do you call a person who keeps on talking when people are no longer interested?
HAROLD: A teacher.

Choosing to Change

Everything can be taken away from a man but one thing:
the last of human freedoms—to choose one's attitude
in any given set of circumstances.
Viktor Frankl[68]

∽

"I had no choice. I just had to have that drink."

"I couldn't help it. He was in my face, and I couldn't stand it. I had to hit him."

Is this all there is? Is this how humans are programmed to live? In the case of addiction, it might seem so. We are powerless over the addiction and find it almost impossible to break free from its effects, although we may know they are disastrous. In the co-dependent seat, we're not much better off. Over time—perhaps a lifetime—we've been acting and reacting a certain way, and it's almost impossible to change, although we experience disastrous consequences if we don't.

But that's NOT all. We hear of people who have overcome tremendous odds to make a good life for themselves. People with addictions sometimes break free and live sane, happy lives. Some people are so obsessed with and consumed by the addicted person that one could almost say they are addicted to the addicted person, and yet they manage to change into individuals of serenity and joy. How? Could it be because they begin to more carefully choose their thoughts and one at a time replace the negative with the positive?

---

[68]Viktor Frankl, *Man's Search for Meaning* (Boston: Beacon Press, 2006). Frankl (1905–1939), Austrian Jewish neurologist and psychiatrist, Holocaust survivor. Founder of Logotherapy.

Like this:

As a teen, I read about Dr. Freud[69] who told us there was, below our conscious thinking mind, a dank, dark basement full of garbage: rinds and pits, green, fuzzy bologna, stinking, maggoty cheese. This was just below the surface and could ooze up any time.

Then there was Dr. Peale,[70] the chubby, smiley-faced preacher who told us of the power of positive thinking to change our lives for the better.

Later I read that if you think positive thoughts 51% of the time, you tip the balance and you begin to get better. I started watching my thoughts and realized I wasn't thinking positive even 10% of the time, maybe not even 1%. No wonder I was a mess. I began to make an effort—sometimes—to choose thoughts of love, kindness, joy, and got a little better.

At a new job, I became aware that at my lunch table sat the two most negative people in the organization. They fed each other's negativity as they ate their sandwiches. I enjoyed the people and the talk but sensed it wasn't good for me, so ate elsewhere most of the time.

I began to be more careful of what was on my TV and cut down on the crime shows with the mean, ugly behavior, even comedies with mean, ugly behavior. People being nice to each other may seem boring, but it doesn't churn up the guts.

I'd come a long way but still wasn't there. Something was missing. The biggest problem in my life was alcoholism and there was no one to talk to about it. If my kids brought it up, I grudgingly discussed it with them—as little as possible. Otherwise I totally clammed up.

In *Reader's Digest* there was an article about Al-Anon, saying people could learn to live with a spouse's alcoholism. Crazy, I said, these people are SICK, no one should live with someone's alcoholism, they should stop it, make it go away, control it. (Yeah, right.)

Finally I did get to Al-Anon. I don't remember the names of the people at the meeting or the topics discussed. I only

[69] Sigmund Freud (1856–1939), Austrian Jewish psychiatrist, best known for psychoanalysis.
[70] Norman Vincent Peale (1898–1993), Protestant minister and author, most famous book *The Power of Positive Thinking*.

remember it was like coming home. Everything I thought might be true or had sensed was real was being validated. It's not like this for everybody. A different meeting probably would have been different for me. But right then I felt like a traveler in a foreign land who suddenly hears his native language and is home. What took me so long?

Jeanie, Al-Anon member

If Al-Anon is that beneficial, why don't more people belong? After all, there are "no dues or fees and the only requirement for membership is the compulsive drinking of a family member or friend." We say there are no dues or fees. And financially this is true, but there is a cost. We need to use the information we get there as well as share our experiences and feelings with the other members. And that can be a difficult thing to do at first. Here choice is a factor. Many of us choose not to do anything ourselves because it's not our problem. Really? If someone else's problem causes us sleepless nights, ghastly stomachaches, and the inability to concentrate, hasn't it become our problem?

Of course Al-Anon is not the only tool we can use to shape our lives for the better. Counseling can be helpful, especially with a counselor who is familiar with the family disease of alcoholism. Even physical changes such as an exercise program can help. Our physical and mental/emotional states are quite intertwined.

We get to choose what, if any, changes to make. You might guess that a good time for us to make major decisions or start a change in our lives would not be until we are in excruciating pain, like from a toothache. Better to put the decision on hold until we've seen the dentist. But deciding NOT to decide is, in itself, a decision.

Most of our choices have very little long-term impact. Deciding what to wear today is not like deciding what career to pursue. Deciding what to have for dinner is not like deciding what changes we may need to make in our overall health habits. Each day we experience a batch of small, seemingly inconsequential decisions. Our physical and emotional states can throw a monkey wrench in our success with these small decisions. The acronym HALT can help us recognize when we're not likely to make good decisions.

HALT = Hungry Angry Lonely Tired

If we're hungry, we can eat, maybe after asking, "Am I hungry because I haven't eaten all day or because I'm craving a double chocolate fudge sundae?" There is a difference.

If we're angry, we may have discovered what works best to diffuse the anger. We may punch a pillow—some say a waterbed works best—or run, lift weights, or do some other physical activity. We may call a friend, someone who will listen without judgment.

If we're lonely, we can make a phone call. The beauty of Al-Anon and other 12-Step programs is that each meeting has a list of phone numbers of people to call; if the first person is not available, go down the list. This can also work when we are angry. There was a woman who had plenty to say to her husband—but it was not in her best interest to say it. So she would call a trusted friend with, "I need to pretend you are my husband. $F@&* !! *&^$&* +*&%$@!!!! Thanks. I feel much better. Bye."

If we're tired, the obvious solution is to take a nap. But that's not so easy in our sleep-deprived society. If there's a work deadline or if the kids are clamoring for attention, we may not have the luxury of a real nap. Sometimes the best we can do is to take a few minutes to sit quietly and breathe deeply.

Is it realistic to see a situation in a different way? The glass half full instead of half empty? Think of Agnes Gonxha Bojaxhiu, better known as Mother Theresa. The average tourist to Calcutta in 1946 saw only poverty and filth and despair. Agnes saw an opportunity to serve and inspire others to service.

Remember Dr. Frankl's words, speaking from the perspective of the concentration camps, that everything can be taken away but one thing: the choice of one's attitude in any given set of circumstances. Here's an example:

> The meeting that night started like any other, same faces, same format...and then a young woman came in and sat down. She'd never been there before and no one ever saw her again. She had to come to a meeting, she said, she needed to make some sense out of what had happened.

> She and her boyfriend had turned their lives around, they had stopped drinking and drugging and were going to get married. After a short vacation, they were coming down a mountain road and were hit by a drunk driver. The fellow was killed instantly; she, herself, was unhurt.

> We all sat in stunned silence until Leslie spoke. Leslie was a regular at that meeting and usually had something funny to say. She began, "I don't know what to say. It happened. You can't change that. You can only choose what to do with it." That started a discussion of attitude. We were not as eloquent as Dr. Frankl, but everyone had something to say

154

about the only choice being the choice of how to respond. To me, this seemed like useful information and I filed it away in the recesses of my mind.

Some time later—was it months or years?—our son died. The wisdom from that meeting came up through the fog of pain and despair, that the only choice was how to respond. It occurred to me that the best advertisement I could ever give for my spiritual programs would be the way I dealt with this experience. I did not always handle it well. But, for the most part, I kept open and didn't shut down and crawl into a hole, as I once would have. I gratefully accepted the help offered and asked for what I needed. Sometimes I thought of this as a learning experience, maybe even a teaching experience.

A friend told my husband he didn't know how he could stand it and my husband replied, "What choice do I have?" Actually, he was aware of his choice of how to respond.

Al-Anon member

Here's the bottom line from a friend and long-time Al-Anon member:

> I could let it destroy me, or I could grow from it.
> **I CHOSE TO GROW!**
> Dave M.

THESE SHOULD BE IN THE DICTIONARY

ADULT: a person who has stopped growing at both ends and is growing in the middle.

BEAUTY PARLOR: a place where women curl up and dye.

CANNIBAL: someone who is fed up with people.

DUST: mud with the juice squeezed out.

EGOTIST: someone who is usually ME deep in conversation.

HANDKERCHIEF: cold storage.

Is There Any Fun in Dysfunction?

Eventually—Why Not Now?

~

The above was a slogan for Gold Medal Flour from 1907 to the early 1950s. This was an advertising slogan put forth by the head of Pillsbury's advertising agency, whose name was B. S. Bull. (They must be joking, but that's what the site really said.)[71]

Presumably the idea was that eventually you would use this flour, so why not jump on the bandwagon now? Don't know how well the slogan worked, but Pillsbury was satisfied enough to keep it for nearly fifty years.

Could this slogan apply to something other than flour? You bet it could—the recovery from addiction.

People in addiction recovery will tell you how much better life is with the program, whether the program is Alcoholics Anonymous, Narcotics Anonymous, Gamblers Anonymous, or any 12-Step program. Al-Anon members say that they are better off with the program than they would be without it, even if the family is not yet free from addiction. How can this be?

As with AA meetings, it's surprising to hear the laughter coming through the Al-Anon doors. What do these people have to laugh about? Many folks who have been around the meeting rooms "many 24 hours" have a serenity, a *joi de vivre* to be envied.

---

[71] General Mills Flour, "Our Heritage," http://www.gmiflour.com/gmflour/ourheritage.aspx.

A friend speaks of being "happy, joyous, and free." Aren't "happy" and joyous" the same? He didn't know; he just liked the "Happy, Joyous, and Free" sign right above the "Coffee, 25 cents" sign he'd seen at his first AA meeting.

Is it possible to get, even for a moment, beyond the agony of addiction to glimpse a future of joy and freedom? And perhaps a bit of fun? If it will happen eventually, we could try to feel it now. An excellent Al-Anon saying is "How important is it?" Some things are not important enough to waste time and energy on. We need to let them go.

There is a high rate of divorce among couples who are raising children with chronic or catastrophic illnesses. The grinding strain of being on watch, of sublimating the needs of their other children to those of the stricken child has sent many loving couples to divorce court.

One woman whose son has Asperger's syndrome was asked how she had avoided this. She said her Mormon belief in the eternal, everlasting nature of the family gave her a perspective of "What will this matter in 10,000 years?"

To see possible future humor in a situation can help us avoid some stress. To reflect back on times when something did turn out to be funny years later may help us do that, just like this:

> There is no one more insecure, more wrapped up in self, more convinced of being the only one who ever felt this way, than a teenager. Interestingly, this is a feeling common to many co-dependents.

> My 10th grade boyfriend went to the rich kids high school. He invited me to go to a school hayride Friday night. What do you wear to a hayride? Blue jeans, plaid shirt, boots, of course. I was dropped off at the boyfriend's house and was horrified to see the fellow and two strange girls, both wearing lovely skirts and cashmere sweaters, looking totally glamorous. I felt like a dung-covered Cinderella cleaning the stables for the princesses. Never say things can't get worse. Uh-oh. I passed gas. Not a little fluff but a huge, rip-roaring explosion!

> Maybe I mercifully went into shock: I have no recollection of anything after that. A day or two later, the boy called and asked for his ring back. I gladly gave it to him. I didn't want to see any of those people again.

Several decades have passed and people in my age group are instructed/commanded to get a colonoscopy. If you've ever had one of those, you know that afterwards, to be released to go home, you must pass gas. So the room is filled with patients striving to do just that. Then I think back to the boy and girls from the rich kids high school. AND NOW I LAUGH!

A little boy went up to his father and asked:
"Dad, where did my intelligence come from?"
The father replied. "Well, son, you must have got it
from your mother, 'cause I still have mine."

An old man goes to the wizard to ask him if he can
remove a curse he has been living with for the last forty years.
The wizard says, "Maybe, but you will have to tell
me the exact words that were used to put the curse on you."'
The old man says without hesitation, "I now pronounce you man and wife."

A man is recovering from surgery when the
surgical nurse appears and asks him how he is feeling.
"I'm OK but I didn't like the four-letter words
the doctor used in surgery," he answered.
"What did he say?" asked the nurse.
"Oops!"

The graveside service had just barely finished when there
was massive clap of thunder, followed by a tremendous bolt of l
ightning, accompanied by even more thunder rumbling in the distance.
The little old man, the husband of the deceased, looked at the
pastor and calmly said, "Well, she's there."

It's Not What I'm Eating...It's What's Eating Me!

Stop being eaten and start living!
Len and Daffy

~

We hope that by now you have gained some insight into what has been happening in your life and the positive changes you might make. We hope you feel it is worth the effort to progress from Victim to Survivor. Remember that FREE help is available at the many 12-Step programs available almost everywhere, including online. Al-Anon and AA are the most common and are the easiest to find. They can work wonders, but *only if you are ready to work with them.*

Most of us have seen those neat canes that have a seat on them that let users take some of the weight off of their legs and rest. This is a great improvement over a mere walking aid, but it is not the best for stability, and it still requires some work to remain upright. Certainly a chair with three or four legs is a better solution. So it is with recovery from stress. A stool with more legs will allow us to be more stable and secure. (Is this another way of describing serenity?) The legs may be a sponsor, counselor, rehab program, family support—you get the idea.

We hope you are reaching out and asking for help when necessary. We hope you are spending less time on the Pity Pot.

It's all right to sit on your Pity Pot every now and again. Just be sure to flush when you are finished.
Debbie Macomber[72]

May you practice the useful skill of living one day at a time—sometimes it's more like one hour at a time. Sometimes even shorter!

...I do not ask to see the distant scene/
One step enough for me.
John Henry Newman,[73] "Lead, Kindly Light"

May you come to appreciate the 12 Steps and consider using them on a daily basis to improve your life. May you begin to rid yourself of resentments and attitudes that don't work to your advantage. May you see possibilities even in disappointments.

Remember that not getting what you want is sometimes a wonderful stroke of luck.
The Dalai Lama[74]

Do remember that it's not what you're eating—it's what's eating you. STOP being eaten. START LIVING!
We wish you joy, happiness, success, and most of all, serenity. May your Higher Power smile on you and lead you always.

Len and Daffy

The authors may be contacted at lvdippold@gmail.com.

---

[72] Debbie Macomber (b. 1948), U.S. author of romance novels.
[73] John Henry Newman (1801–1890), British Cardinal, beatified 2010.
[74] The Dalai Lama (b. 1935), spiritual leader of Tibetan Buddhists.